Worthy of Trust

Dedication

This book is dedicated with sincere thanks to those at Alleyn's School, St. Barnabas Church and further afield who read or heard (knowingly or unknowingly) draft extracts from this book.

And as ever to my family and to Philip Ralli of Highland Books.

It would not have been completed without your patience and kindness.

Anthony Buckley, Dulwich 2016

Worthy of Trust

Anthony Buckley

Highland

First published in 2016 by Highland Books, 2 High
Pines, Knoll Road, Godalming, GU7 2EP, England

ISBN-13: 978-1-897913-93-2

ISBN-10: 1-897913-93-1

Ebook ISBN: 978-1-909690-93-6

Printed and bound by
CPI Books (UK) Ltd, Croydon, CR0 4YY

Contents

Section I, Thinking about Trust

Section II, What Can We Trust Jesus To Do?

Section III, Evidence, Dreams and a New Beginning

Printed Acknowledgments

Other works cited:

Reflection 7

Venerable Bede: *Ecclesiastical History of the English People*

Reflection 13

Eugene Peterson, Scripture taken from *The MESSAGE*. Copyright © 1993,1995,1996,2000,20001,2002, Used by permission of the NavPress Publishing Group

C. F. Alexander: *Once in Royal David's City,* 1848

Reflection 21

G.K Chesterton: *The Sign Of The Broken Sword,* The Complete Father Brown Stories, Penguin 2012

Reflection 22

Corrie Ten Boom: *The Hiding Place,* Hodder & Stoughton 1971

Reflection 24

G.K Chesterton: *The Flying Stars,* The Complete Father Brown Stories, Penguin 2012

John Pollock: *Newton the Liberator,* Kingsway Publications 2000

Reflection 26

C. S. Lewis: *The Last Battle,* Fontana Lion 1980

Reflection 27

Louis Berkhof: *Systematic Theology,* Banner of Truth 1984

William Chatterton Dix: *Alleluia! Sing to Jesus!* 1867

Reflection 36

The words of Martin Luther King Jr. Edited by Coretta Scott King, Robson Books 1983

Reflection 38

Josephus: *Antiquities of the Jews*

Suetonius: *The Lives of the Twelve Caesars*

Tacitus: *Annals*

Pliny: *Letters*

Introduction

In this short book there are forty reflections about trust. They are offered not as definitive statements but rather as brief ideas to spark further thinking. It may be helpful to allow time to consider each one, thinking about where you agree or disagree, and what you may wish to do with what you have read.

The central theme is that whenever we talk about trusting someone there is an inevitable, often unspoken, second half of the sentence: there is something specific that we are trusting this person *to do*.

This is true of all our relationships and the same question arises for those interested in Christian faith. Christians talk rather a lot about trusting in Jesus, but what does that mean? What do they trust Jesus *to do?*

Some of the reflections are based around two characters, Alex and Thomas. Thomas seems to be particularly interested in issues around trust; as the book continues his identity becomes a little clearer.

If any small phrase catches your attention and is helpful to you in your understanding of trust, given and received, then the author will be grateful indeed. He has much to learn in this area himself, hence the need to write the book.

Section 1,
Thinking
about Trust

Reflection 1

A restless beginning to a walk

> *There are times when I long*
> *For a world refreshed*
> *With hope restored, renewed*
> *Where truth and trust grow strong*
> *Once more*
> *And fear is lost in love*

I pushed the paper across the desk with resignation and frustration. It had not been a good morning. And now this poem was not working either. What was I trying to say? Was it a plaintive cry or a call to arms? I looked out of the window and saw the hill that I had seen so often but had never visited. It seemed a good day for a walk.

At the top of the hill there was a grassy glade. I sat with my back against a tree and looked around. A group was gathering and they seemed to be preparing for some sort of campaign. Some were smiling and some were grim-faced. Bags were being fastened and hitched on to shoulders, boot laces were being tied tighter. It was a warm and fresh morning.

I heard snatches of conversations and caught the exchanges, spoken and unspoken. It seemed that the next stage of the campaign was a walk down the hill and through the woods. It was uncertain terrain. There would no doubt be need for company, conversation and assistance. Something caught my eye and I looked up in time to see a bird flying across the glade.

"What are you thinking?" A young man had walked across and was standing next to me.

I am not one of those who can slip easily into relaxed conversations with strangers but I did not feel as guarded as I would usually be. Perhaps this was an unusual place. I wondered why I had not visited it before, even though its outline had always seemed familiar. I found myself replying:

"I am wondering what it means to prepare for a journey alongside companions such as these. I am wondering how they know they can trust each other."

"This is a question that is good to ask," my new companion replied. "My name is Thomas. Would you like to know more?"

His directness and assurance were disconcerting, and so, if I'm honest, was the topic. Trust has been both a comforting and a disturbing word for me. I could think of friendships that have been full of trust but, equally vividly, there was that time when someone I had trusted badly let me down. And there were the times when I had damaged friends' trust in me. I have let more people down than I care to remember.

Perhaps I was thinking about all this because trust was more on my mind than I realised. That in itself felt rather unsettling. Or perhaps it was the hill. And so I simply nodded. Thomas sat down on the grass and continued:

"Do you see how this large group is divided into much smaller groups, preparing to walk down the hill? In these smaller groups the key theme, as you have guessed, is the kind of trust that exists between the members. The three questions they are asking about each other are these:

* Can I trust them to care for me?
* Can I trust them to be able to help me, to make a difference?
* Can I trust them to trust me in turn?"

"You seem very sure about all this," I said, aware of how defensive I was now sounding. "I think I need you to explain a little more about those three questions."

"I would be pleased to do so," said Thomas. "May I ask your name?"

"Alex." I replied.

Reflection 2

Trusting someone who cares

"Alex, look at that group getting ready over there," said Thomas. "Look at the way they glance or smile at each other. They like being together. There is genuine affection. If you are in that group, you know that you are cared for.

"It is not selfish to want to be cared for and to be valued, it is a healthy recognition that we need external affirmation to help us flourish. It makes sense to want to trust someone who is on our side and who has our best interests at heart.

"This does not mean we want to be favoured. It would be too narrow to trust someone who is never willing to affirm others whilst apparently always keen to affirm us. We know that our well-being is tied up with that of the group. It is not enough for you to be the only one to play your clarinet well, you want the whole orchestra to sound good. For the orchestra to succeed each person needs to receive the right support and guidance so each can play their part as best they can. Deep down we understand that if our trusted friend is truly on our side then sometimes they may need to speak difficult truths so we can play better, we trust them to care enough to do that.

"Trusting someone who truly cares includes knowing that the person is willing to listen to our whole situation. If not, there may arise conversations like these: 'I wanted her to chat with me about my career prospects, but she never even asked what stage my children were at in school, and whether they could move easily'. 'He listens so he can say he listens, but he is not really interested in what he hears.' 'He does not care that I play hockey. He once learnt to trampoline and that's all he wants to talk about. In fact, I rather think he would prefer it if I stopped playing hockey altogether.' 'She pretends she is listening to me but all the time her eyes are darting around, seeing if there is someone more interesting in the room.' 'He kept asking me lots of questions, but somehow it seemed to be more for his interest than for my benefit.' We want to be able to trust someone who cares for us as we are, and will listen to our story as it is."

Sitting on the grass in the morning sun I remembered and honoured those whom I could trust to care for me, those who had truly listened to as much as I was willing to share. And then I considered those whom I thought had cared, but who later I had painfully realised were following their own agenda. As if reading my thoughts, Thomas continued:

"People's motives are always going to be slightly mixed. But you would be surprised at how many continue wanting to trust people who do not really care for them at all."

I nodded at that. I wondered how he knew I played the clarinet. And that my experiences of trying to be part of an orchestra were, to say the least, somewhat mixed.

Reflection 3

Trusting someone who is able to help

"Look over there," said Thomas. "The group that is full of different ages. They all care for each other, from the youngest to the oldest, the weakest to the strongest, they trust each other to *do something* as the campaign continues. The care for each other will be expressed in action."

"I don't like the idea of children being involved in a campaign, if that means some sort of battle." I said, rather shortly.

"It is not the sort of battle you are used to thinking about." Thomas replied. "But it is a battle nonetheless and everyone is part of it.

"The verb 'trust' always has an object but that object then becomes a subject. When I say 'I trust Henry', the object of the sentence, Henry, then becomes a subject in his own right. I trust Henry *to do something*. When I say 'I trust someone' there is thus always an unspoken question: What do I trust this person to do? We do the same about objects: What do I trust a chair to do? I trust it to support my weight.

"My answer to the question 'What do I trust Henry to do for me?' reveals as much about me as it does about him. It says a great deal about my own desires and about my understanding of who Henry is and what he can offer. Perhaps I trust Henry to make me feel somehow special because he will contemptuously whisper gossip about someone else. Perhaps I trust Mary to be honest, even if the truth is unpalatable. Perhaps I trust Matilda always to look as if she is glad to see me. Perhaps I trust Fred to give comfort and peace.

"I do not trust someone as if they are an inanimate exhibit in a museum, I trust them to be and to do *something*, and what that *something* is will be a central part of what I have in mind when I say that I trust them. To put it simply, I want to be able to trust them to make a difference, to be able to help me.

"The help may be putting up curtains or offering wise words of counsel, it may be a smile or a prayer, a thousand pounds or a challenging insight. It may be something emotional, spiritual or material. The help may not appear to be active; one person may simply be able to smile at me from her armchair as I walk past her window each morning, but that familiar friendly greeting becomes important to me. I trust her to give it.

"To be fair to the person, and to myself, I need to be honest about their capacity to be able to deliver what I am expecting. Sometimes I put my trust in someone for something specific and they are not able to provide what I need. Through no fault of theirs they may not be able to give the right support for this particular moment in my life. Addicts may surround themselves with friends who have no idea how to help and have no real desire to do so. Distressed parents sometimes inappropriately burden young children by trusting them for the kind of emotional support that can be given best by those in the adult world.

"If you are going to trust someone, you want them to be able to help and you will need to discover whether they have the right resources to do so."

I interrupted. "But there are toddlers and children in that group. What role can they possibly play?"

"The older ones trust the younger ones to receive help, to respond with smiles, sleep or tears in the way that honest children do. They are not trusting them to carry the heavy bags. But they are trusting them to be excited about an outing and an adventure, shoulder-rides and squirrels, and they are trusting them to know they are loved."

"Shoulder-rides and squirrels do not fit into my idea of a battle," I said.

"It all depends what sort of battle we need to fight," he replied. "Whether it is reading a map, carrying a bag or telling good jokes, everyone has a role, and they are trusted to carry it out. They do not trust the best joke-teller to be the best map-reader, or the child to carry an adult on her back. When you think about trusting someone, ask yourself what you are trusting them to do.

"As to the battle, Alex, remember your poem you were writing this morning. What were you reaching for? Were you not talking about a campaign? Restoring, renewing, refreshing? Those are words of action and purpose; obstacles may have to be overcome to achieve them, difficult decisions made, perhaps even battles fought against despair and isolation."

For some reason I did not feel I could ask Thomas how he knew about the poem. I could not quite remember the words I had jotted down and it was rather disconcerting that he knew them better than I did.

But I could remember the sense of longing that lay behind them.

Reflection 4

Trusting someone who trusts us

I was still sitting against the tree. I plucked absent-mindedly at some grass and decided to move the conversation on. "I can see that a group will work when people trust each other to care and trust each other to do what they are truly able to do. But your third question implies that trust should be given to those who trust you in return. What do you mean by that?"

Thomas replied: "In all genuine relationships the trust and respect work in both directions. If I trust someone I hope that they will trust and respect me in return. I would like to trust them to see me as a real person, not a statistic or completely powerless. They are not speaking to an answering-machine or a robot, they are speaking to me. And I need to know they value me as such. I would like them to trust me to be able to respond to their care for me

"The woman in the green sweater over there is trusted to lead her group down the hill. Part of their trust in her is knowing that she trusts them to follow. She is not going to bundle them into bags and carry them down, she trusts them to respond and act for themselves. Some in the group may decide she is wrong and they may choose to go on another path. They have trusted her to give them that freedom.

"Alex, I want to trust people who will respect me. They care for me and help me but they are not going to take over my whole life for me, or forget that my story matters in its own right. I want to trust someone who will trust me to stand on my own feet, even if I need lots of support to do so.

"And when I am completely helpless, when I am very old or very young, I still want them to trust that my humanity has a dignity and value beyond price. Whatever my needs may be, I still want to have an identity, an importance and a purpose in their eyes. I want to trust someone who believes that.

"So when you think about whom you want to trust, you may want to think about whether they respect you enough to trust you, to value you, to take you seriously. Is that not a fair thing for you to consider?"

Reflection 5

Why do I sometimes get it wrong?

Thomas turned and looked at me again: "What are you thinking?" he asked.

"I am remembering those times when I have chosen to trust the wrong people. And I am wondering why I made those mistakes." And I looked at the ground.

Thomas said nothing for a few moments and then replied: "Sometimes it is about not knowing what we really want and so we flail around, trusting people to give us what we think we need whereas our real needs lie elsewhere. Sometimes it is because as children our trust was broken by a parent and we may have become over-cautious or over-hasty to trust anything or anyone that looks like a parent. Sometimes we trust someone because they really want us to trust them and we want to please them, but the trust is misplaced and they cannot give us what we hoped. Sometimes we simply don't know the person as well as we thought we did.

"And we need to remember that no one is perfect and in every relationship there is the likelihood of feeling let down. Our ability to cope with the inevitable flaws in our relationships becomes an important issue in its own right. We may need to be challenged quite deeply about our levels of awareness, honesty and forgiveness."

I decided to put the barriers back up and move the conversation to something new.

"Well, that has all been very interesting. I assume I am here because I am meant to join this battle too, whatever it is. I better get on and decide what group I should join."

Thomas smiled. "Before you rush in, looking for those whom you think you can trust best, remember that they will equally be looking at you. They will want to trust you as much as you want to trust them. Are you good at caring for people? What can they trust you to do for them? What are you willing to trust them to do themselves?

"We think long and hard about whom we trust, or at least we should do; we should equally think carefully about those who want to trust us. And how best we can meet their expectations. There are important questions to be faced about ourselves and others, our relationships and our mutual needs. The answers can be clearer at some points in our lives than at others. Genuine trust takes time to build."

Reflection 6

*Trust is about ideologies
as well as people*

"Something I should add before you join the others," said Thomas, "is that there are different hilltops with different forces gathering and you should take that into account as you choose what group is right for you. Over there (he pointed across a wooded valley to another hill) there is an inward-looking circle that wants to go to the mountains and will despise and condemn any others they meet on the way. Or over there is a group that will go to the fertile lands to the west and will ignore anyone else they see on the way, pretending they do not exist. Over there is one that sees itself as an army, battling for justice wherever it goes and who do not mind being distracted to other paths if there is injustice to be fought.

"If you look further you will see a myriad of groups, each one has its own destination and its own values. There are very different ideas as to what the struggle is and how it should be fought. You need to decide whether the aims and values of this team, on this hill, are worthy of your trust.

"We believe in goals, values, even attitudes as much as we trust people. The ideas we credit will shape and guide our thinking. Someone trusting racism as holding the correct attitude to people of different colour will live very differently to someone who is not racist. Attitudes drive our behaviour: even, say, our everyday choice of baby-sitter could (consciously or unconsciously) reflect certain of our opinions or biases.

"To take another example: if I choose to admire sexist comedy, trusting this interpretation of life to have something clever to say, then I may find I increasingly think or say sexist comments myself, and my attitude will become flawed and warped. Or if I constantly watch a talent show where the producers subtly encourage the audience to mock a weak participant then I will need to be aware if this way of treating people is growing within me, and ask whether it is an attitude which detracts from my personal credibility.

"What ideas do we live by? Where did they come from? What underlying wisdom do we use to determine which are trustworthy? We are constantly exposed to different views about how we should be living our lives, about how the world 'really' works. Whenever we watch or read, listen or look, we are exposed to an underlying ideology and we will be making a judgement as to whether it is one we wish to share or not. We are making a decision about its trustworthiness.

"When we were children the values in our homes provided our first reference points and as we grew up there was probably a time when we questioned them. Many people then cheerfully and thankfully realise that much of this foundational ideology was good and take it on for themselves. But sometimes the growing adult sees that some of the foundation may have been unhelpful and they need to build a new one for themselves. This is often a courageous and difficult journey but it is better to change to the good than stay with the bad, however accustomed we are to it.

"And of course it is never an issue of purely good and bad, our backgrounds are inevitably mixed. It is a healthy and humbling thought that whatever reference points we choose to live by will be questioned by the next generation in turn.

"And don't forget that ideas as well as people will promise something. It is a reminder of our second question: What are we trusting this person (or philosophy) *to do*? Let me give examples: Cynthia is part of a group that trusts in good friendships to bring fulfilment, Herbert is brought up to trust money to bring happiness, Flora decides that being sexually attractive will be enough to get what she wants, Michael wants to stay looking as young as he can for as long as possible because that fits in with the culture he thinks he is part of. Some put trust in learning, religion, having a quiet life, money, fitness or career success. Others trust the idea that furthering a political cause or being a responsible member of a family will bring the most satisfaction.

"There are two risks. The first is that we may not achieve what we aim for. Michael's hair will turn grey, however much he tries to hide it. Cynthia's best friends may let her down. Herbert's money may disappear.

"The second risk is this: What does it mean for the person if they achieve their aim, as articulated by their ideology, but then find that it does not deliver the achievement or satisfaction that they expected?"

I shrugged, while beginning to wonder if I might ever get up and join the others, or even if I wanted to. But Thomas was in full flow.

"We are surrounded by different claims on our trust. Every advertiser and song writer, every news editor and internet commentator, every teacher and parent, script writer and politician, faith leader and fashion designer is saying: 'Trust me, and trust my view of how the world works.' It is likely, Alex, that the voices that you have chosen to follow, whether belonging to individuals or philosophies, shape your values, thoughts and behaviour more than you realise."

"That is quite a big thing to say." I broke in. This man did seem to talk a lot. And I was not used to listening, or to being put on the spot (if I was? It was hard quite to know). "We have only just met!"

"There will be a bigger issue I will need to address," said Thomas calmly. "Let us pause for a moment."

He got up, stretched contentedly, and went over to chat to one of the groups. It seemed he knew them already. I stood up but preferred to stay on my own, walking to an edge of the glade and gazing through the trees, watching the light and shadows settling and resting on the quiet ground.

Turning over the conversations in my mind I wondered which parts had disturbed me, which I found comfortable and which simply felt too close to home. These last I had blocked, and thus, perhaps, had neither comforted or disturbed me.

Memories of others, memories of myself. I was not at all sure I wanted to continue and realised that this pause meant I could slip away – or maybe Thomas would slip away – and the conversation could stop. And I realised that this pause was being given so that this choice could be made.

I looked back and saw that Thomas was back at my tree. He was not looking at me but I sensed he was waiting to see if I would return.

Reflection 7

A hall and a sparrow

"Thank you for coming back," said Thomas.

"Nothing much to lose, only some time."

"Perhaps," said Thomas, with a slight smile.

"I want to say," I said, in as business-like and calm voice as possible, "I don't do the deep personal stuff, certainly not with strangers but not really with anyone, either. Whatever the big thing is you want to talk about, I will only stay as long as I wish."

"Of course, and rightly so, and no one is forcing you to stay. No-one made you come back to the tree. But now you are back, let us see where we have got to. Would you agree that, above all, we want to be able to trust something or someone that will see us through?"

I nodded cautiously, that seemed fair enough. Thomas continued: "But what does 'through' mean? That will depend on your view of the landscape, where you think you are heading and what battle you think you are fighting. Your choice of people and ideologies to trust will largely be determined by what you perceive your journey to be. If you are travelling across an ocean, you require a ship's captain, not a bus driver. Do we have to consider what is the right journey? What or who is then the right guide?

"There is one particular divide in the road that will need to be considered and this is the big issue I mentioned. It is to do with your perception of yourself. If you believe that all you are is material, is physical, then you may feel that the priority is seeing yourself, those closest to you and those whom you are concerned about, safely through emotional and physical life. The road will have a final destination and you will want to trust people who can meet these concerns as you journey towards it.

"If you see yourself as more than material, that you are more than atoms, then you will be looking for something that will see you safely through what then becomes a more complex landscape – the complexity increases because this point of view is likely to include some level of belief in spiritual reality and perhaps a belief in eternity itself. You will find yourself considering a different destination, and a different guide will be needed.

"The roads at times look very similar and any differences may not be immediately apparent to an external observer or indeed to yourself. If I am a materialist and part of my thinking is that it is of core importance to be on good terms with my neighbours, because that helps all of us feel happier and safer, then I will do my best to be courteous on all occasions. But courtesy is equally considered in the best religions to be an important part of a life that is to be lived for ever, whether or not such courtesy leads to happiness and safety in the short term. The materialist may wish to save the environment because that leads to peace, beauty and health; the religious person may wish to save the environment because they believe that their deity wishes them to do so. Two friends may thus be acting outwardly in the same way, but the underlying (and sometimes unconscious) motivation may ultimately be different. From the outside it may look like the same behaviour on the same road but the materialist and the more-than-materialist (if I can put it that way) are on different journeys and are trusting different guides.

"Do you know the story of the hall and the sparrow? Let me take you back to the 7th century. The historian Bede writes about these two different roads when he tells the story of a visitor, Paulinus, speaking to King Edwin of Northumbria about Christianity. One of Edwin's advisors was listening to the visitor, and said something like this to the king:

> 'Reflect, my king. When we think about
> our life on earth and then think about that
> time of which we have no knowledge, we
> can think of a sparrow flying through this

banqueting-hall, where you are dining on a winter's day with your lords and advisors. Inside, the hall is warmed and lit by a comforting fire; outside, the winter storms of rain or snow are raging. This sparrow flies swiftly in through one door of the hall and out through another. While the bird is inside the hall he is away from the winter storms, but after a moment of comfort, he vanishes from sight into the unknown, outer, world from whence he came. Humanity likewise appears on earth for a little while, but of what went before this life or of what follows, we know nothing. If this new teaching can tell us more, it is surely right that we should consider further.'

"Alex, if you believe that all that exists is the 'hall' of this earthly life then your search for the right aspiration or ideology to trust is likely to be different from that of someone who believes it is worth exploring the journey through the hall in the context of what may come afterwards.

"Throughout human history the vast majority of people have felt that there is something more than just the hall, that we are more than material. In recent times there has been a growing, if statistically small, number of those who argue that there is nothing outside, that a person is a collection of chemicals and no more. It is quite an important difference in perception of oneself."

"I have many friends on both sides of this debate, and several in the middle," I responded. "I am not sure I would want to say that any of them particularly behave better according to their choice."

"I am not arguing that they do," replied Thomas. "It is the difference in choosing which journey you feel to be most valid, and thus which guides are to be trusted, that I am trying to highlight."

Reflection 8

Both views have their difficulties

"My friends have such arguments over these things." I said, sadly. And I thought back to hard words and friendships broken.

"Both views are held strongly and neither is straightforward. Perhaps the passion in the arguments is because people grasp the importance, and struggle to grasp the complexity, of the choice," replied Thomas.

"Both views have their difficulties. One difficulty with the theory that all we have is the hall, the physical or material life, is that there is then no underlying reason why anything should ultimately matter. Apart from an appeal to instinct or present pleasure, this view finds it difficult to give any deeper philosophical reason why we should constantly, sacrificially, struggle to do 'good' or what may be the point of achieving the survival of the species (and in this mind-set words like 'should' are best avoided, because there is no overarching justice or morality that can be appealed to).

"This view struggles fully to explain why we find sunsets beautiful, why our heart is filled with a sense of profound injustice (not simply empathy) at the death of a stranger a thousand miles away. It struggles to offer a convincing account of why we paint pictures. It struggles with a lack of ultimate, unbreakable, reason for hope, meaning and purpose. It struggles with the implication that people's processes of thought might only be based on mechanical and unguided movements of physical particles – how can these 'thoughts' be trusted? These are intellectual struggles that many of my materialist friends face with dignity and integrity. They know they are not easy issues.

"But those who believe there is something outside the hall equally face challenges. Is there genuine evidence that there is something more than the material? Is this just not wishful thinking? If there is a heaven or a God, why are they not more obvious? If there is something or someone better out there, then why is so much of what is in here so miserable? And how do we handle the truth that rather a lot of people who believe in a spiritual reality have used this belief as a justification to do terrible things to others? Why do people who believe that there might be something out there divide and disagree so much with each other? These are not easy issues, either.

"Both choices have their intellectual challenges but it is unarguable that most of the world has been, and is, religious: most people have, generally, taken the view that there is something outside the hall. And it is interesting that Christianity, the belief system that has become the most widespread of all, has at its heart the concept of *trust*. And that is where our conversation began."

"I am interested in trust, like anyone else," I agreed, "and I am still thinking about what you said earlier about finding the right kind of trust. But it seems quite a jump to move to religion."

"I am not sure it is a big jump," said Thomas. "We all trust ideas and philosophies in the same way we trust individuals. Christianity is one such idea and is the biggest. It would seem worth a look?"

Reflection 9

A book opens...

I think I went rather shame-faced because part of my reluctance to carry on with this discussion was due to my ignorance, I realised I did not know very much about this at all. Thomas looked at me and said (to my surprise, rather self-consciously), "Would you like to read more? I tried writing something about this once." I smiled and nodded. Thomas reached into a bag and brought out an old and tattered book.

Inscribed in the front page were these words: "To those who enquire with open hearts and minds into the trustworthiness of Jesus called the Christ, formerly of Nazareth, briefly of Jerusalem."

I opened the book. Inside was a note:

> Christianity claims not only to be about Jesus but to be about trusting Jesus. In this he is different from other characters in history. People believe that Elizabeth 1st existed but they do not trust her to forgive their sins. Trust in Jesus, belief in Jesus, faith in Jesus - the words are close enough in meaning to be interchangeable for our

purposes - is, according to Christian thinking, how we best receive all that God wants to give us. It is believed that trusting in Jesus is how we connect with what is outside King Edwin's hall as well as giving particular insight into what is going on inside.

Jesus never wrote a book, led an army or ran a country. He did not travel far and he did not live long. But during his life and immediately after his death people were saying extraordinary things about him, and they continue to do so.

There is a difference between Christianity and the other major religions at this point. In Christianity we are asked to consider what it is to trust a person, not a system of laws or a book. (In contrast, for example, to Islam where the Prophet points to the Koran, it is all about the Book. In Christianity the Bible points to Jesus, it is all about the Person.) "Trust in God; trust also in me", says Jesus in that emotionally charged and fearful evening before he was arrested.

But what is this trust meant to mean? As I explained on the hilltop, we trust people to do different things. I trust my bank manager to look after my bank account, I do not trust her to be an expert on Elvis Presley. She might or she might not, it is incidental and unimportant to her core calling. I do not trust Jesus to be the best acrobat in the Roman Empire and he does not ask me to do so.

Alex, in considering how some of the issues we have been talking about might echo with the life of the son of a Galilean carpenter two thousand years ago I remind you of our three criteria for a healthy relationship of trust.

✓ Trusting someone who cares for us

✓ Trusting someone who is able to help us

✓ Trusting someone who is willing to trust us

Here are twenty-eight readings from the Bible about what trust in this man might look like. They do not tell the whole story, and I am not telling you everything about him, by any means. Sometimes I have not covered the central meaning of these records of glimpses into his words and actions, preferring instead simply to focus on what they say about his trustworthiness. I know it can all feel rather personal but I am used to dealing in 'us' or 'we', I have a twin brother, we often chat like this about these things. You may want to follow up the Bible references and stories yourself.

Something towards the end of this note sparked a memory in my mind. I could not place it. I was also aware that I had no idea where my old Bible, given at school, might be. Never mind. I might be able to get through without one. I said goodbye to my new friend and walked back down the hill. I would look at his book tomorrow.

Section 2, What Can We Trust Jesus To Do?

Reflection 10

Day 1 . . . . . . *.To have time*
Mark 6:21-43
               5

Jairus' daughter was on the point of death. This was desperately sad but some might cynically say it is an opportunity. Healing the daughter of the ruler of the synagogue won't do your cause any harm, Jesus.

But Jesus stops on the way. Someone else reaches out to him and Jesus is not going to be rushed while this needs to be sorted out. He knows that it is not enough for this older woman to be physically healed. She needs to hear the voice of comfort and restoration and that might take time. Trust is about relationship, not achievements. He wants to see her face. So he stops and gives her his full attention.

During those minutes the news comes through that Jairus' daughter has died. For the sake of a conversation with someone considered 'unclean' in her community Jesus had apparently failed in his ministry to one of the most important families in town.

Jesus carries on. And he has time to do what is needed for Jairus' family, too. All the time in the world. The little girl is healed and restored. It is a new beginning.

Jesus will not be rushed and he will not march to our timetable. We tend to want results quickly, or to arrive at a particular time that exactly matches our self-created plans. It is as if we believe we ought to be able to control the future. We are sometimes tempted to think that our dreams will only become reality if our timetable is met and that if God had any sense at all he would know our agenda and get things done on time.

If we are living in the light of eternity, we need to remember that the important issues are to do with what sort of people we are becoming, not what steps on the career ladder have to be met by when. If it takes five years for us to become a little more loving to our neighbour, then the five years is well spent.

Sometimes we feel that time has been wasted. Perhaps when struggling through a dark time we may feel that nothing happened at all or that we have missed unrepeatable opportunities. Jesus is less scared of the passing of time than we are. If it is right to happen, then, when the time is right, it will happen. Jesus, steeped in the Old Testament, would have been very aware of the promise given by the prophet Joel "I will repay you for the years the locusts have eaten." At one stage, frustrated by the narrow focus of the Pharisees, Jesus says: "Before Abraham was born, I am." One of the implications of this extraordinary statement is that because he is outside linear time he can ensure that nothing, past, present and future, is wasted. He has time for us, all the time in the world. The years, the opportunities, that we thought had been eaten by the locusts can be restored.

Reflection 11

Day 2 . . . . *To build, not crush*
John 8:1-11,
Luke 23:32-43

It must have been one of the worst moments of her life. She had been caught committing adultery and was now being dragged very publicly to be judged. Her partner is nowhere to be seen, which seems profoundly unfair. She is all alone. Might she even be stoned? Is this how her young life is to end? She quickly realises that, as well as contempt being expressed for what she has done, she is being used as a pawn to trap this new teacher from Galilee. Perhaps she has heard something of Jesus already and feels even worse that it is in front of him that she will be judged. But he is also known to be somewhat unpredictable, perhaps she begins to allow herself to hope.

Jesus will have none of this public humiliation. He relentlessly and skilfully puts the accusers in their place so they can leave with at least some dignity intact but with much to ponder and it is very clear that they are being dismissed. He then looks at the woman and tells her that he does not condemn her, but points out that a change of lifestyle is needed. It is a moment of deep compassion. Protecting her from the mob. Loving her as she is but loving her too much to want to leave her as she is.

***

For this thief, justice has spoken; any last hopes of freedom are dashed. There is to be no last minute reprieve. And now the excruciating pain of crucifixion. In the agony his mind stays clear enough to remember that, as far as he can tell, the criminal next to him is no criminal at all and, remembering further, perhaps is rather more than just another innocent victim of injustice. He asks for mercy and for hope: "Jesus, remember me when you come into your kingdom."

Jesus answers. He does not say: "Not now, you're too late, you think you've got troubles, you ought to see mine." He responds with words of absolute comfort, power and assurance. Full of compassion, he replies: "I tell you the truth, today you will be with me in paradise."

Whenever we are struggling, vulnerable and fragile we can remember that Jesus is compassionate. Whenever we are feeling strong and in control, we can remember that Jesus is compassionate. We are to receive and give compassion in equal measure.

And so we are to see compassion and gentleness as high callings. We are to be compassionate to others and to ourselves, recognising both the value and the fragility of human nature. St. Paul talked about 'gentleness' being one of the fruit of God's Spirit. Jesus talked about the meek being blessed. When in a position of power, a fundamental question is how we use the said powers. It is a sign of inadequacy and weakness to crush a child, any fool can do that. It takes strength and patience to hold a child safely.

Jesus cared for the woman caught in adultery. He cared for the thief on the cross. He cares equally for us. We can trust him to do so. He is here to build, not crush.

Reflection 12

Day 3 . . . . To know our story
John 4:1-30

A trip to collect water was turning into an unexpected encounter. The game-changing moment in the conversation was when she realised that the stranger knows her story. He knows her complex past and her current condition and still seems entirely comfortable with asking her for water and chatting about faith.

And she had been feeling very different to him: a woman and a man, a Samaritan and a Jew. But still he talks to her, still he wants to affirm that he knows her, still he wants to tell her that he is the one who can bring the satisfaction which eternally refreshes and renews. This must be what she and the world craves.

Jesus knows our stories. He understands all that has happened. He knows the reasons and the backgrounds, he knows which excuses are valid and which are contrived. He did not marginalise the Samaritan woman because of her past. He does not marginalise us.

In response we should accept that our stories matter. If Jesus values and honours them then so should we. This does not mean we look at the past with naïve sentimentality or unquestioning nostalgia, but rather that we recognise its role in shaping what we have become.

And this is not always easy. There may be parts that trouble us or parts that we do understand: Why did I do that? Why did that happen to me? What was going on in the background that shaped those events and situations? It is helpful to try to begin to understand such things but we never see the whole picture and memories can be confused and distorted. As we search back we may find ourselves more uncertain, or we uncover things that rightly need healing but which can still disturb if revealed at the wrong time. Our stories matter so much that sometimes they need to be explored in the presence of a kind and wise friend.

And the story of our neighbour matters and is likewise to be valued. If we are trusting in a Jesus who honours their story, then so should we.

Jesus makes clear that we need have no secrets from him, and in fact we cannot. He knows the parts that are shameful and those that are very good. He knows the sad moments and the confusion. He knows the golden memories of joy. He knows all about the mixed motives. He knows where responsibility truly lies. He knows more about our story, and sees it more clearly, than we do ourselves. And he wants to engage with us.

Reflection 13

Day 4 . . . . To know what it is
to be vulnerable
John 1:14, 6:42

"Is this not Jesus, the son of Joseph, whose father and mother we know?" They asked, implying: "From Nazareth? Really, he is just like one of us." In a sense they were right, Jesus is like one of us. Jesus knows what it is to grow up in a home. He knows what it is to be single and what it is to have friends. What it is to learn and what it is to work. The quiet joys and struggles of being with other people. And so the ordinary is honoured. When we think of Jesus, we remember that he knows what it is to do the washing up. He knows what it is to enjoy a sunset. He knows about relationships, about trust being received well and trust betrayed. Eugene Peterson translates John 1:14 in this way: "The Word became flesh and blood, and moved into the neighbourhood." We can trust him to care for us so much that he is willing to be identified with us.

And Jesus moved into the neighbourhood as a helpless baby, not as a warrior king. He knows what it is to be a toddler and a child. He knows what it is to be a refugee, to be thirsty, to be humiliated, to be punished unjustly, to be betrayed by a friend and to die. He knows what it is to be weak and to be at the mercy of others. He knows what it is for his vulnerability to be seen and to be exploited.

Many of us spend considerable amounts of energy, money or time trying to hide our vulnerability. We may decide not to answer a particular question quite honestly, or choose only to undertake tasks that guarantee success, or projects that, when we fail, we will get enormous plaudits for attempting. We may be so nervous of people's opinion of our appearance that we spend longer preparing our faces for the day ahead than we spend on preparing our hearts and minds. Perhaps we will not face up to a particular truth about ourselves. Deep down we know that we are vulnerable, that we can be hurt if a particular weakness is exposed. So we do our best to cover up.

And sometimes it is right that we do so. There are times when others will exploit our vulnerability. They will use their power to manipulate or denigrate. It can hurt deeply, and Jesus knows that hurt. For some of us, sadly, it can be right to hide, or at least closely protect, parts of our vulnerability.

But we are mistaken if we constantly pretend that we are invulnerable, that we are strong and capable and that everything goes our way. Jesus knew that he did not always have to win (and if he had wanted, he could have won every time). We forget that accepting our vulnerability is liberating. It means we can receive help and support as needed and it means we can be honest. It means we can get on with things without worrying that all will fall apart if any of our fragile defences slip. We can face up to what we are and still face the world. We can be a liberating example, not an oppressive perfectionist model, to those who look to us.

As the Christmas carol has it: "Tears and smiles like us he knew". A first nation Canadian proverb runs "Walk a mile in my moccasins to learn where they pinch". This Jesus whom we are called to trust has walked in our shoes.

Reflection 14

Day 5   .   To know what it is to grieve
John 11:35

Love includes vulnerability and this will include the pain of shared and personal grief. Jesus knew that he was going to restore Lazarus to life, but he does not dance with complacent joy or swagger smugly to the tomb. Grief hangs heavy in the air and he weeps with those who were weeping. In that moment the pain and sorrow had to be faced. The death of Lazarus is a terrible and sad event; it is worth crying about.

Comfort does not always come in words or tears (but sometimes rightly is expressed in both), it can equally come in the glimpse that this sad event *matters* to the other person.

Many of us have already suffered immense sadness in our lives. C.S. Lewis once wrote that grief feels like fear, bringing paralysing and unsettling feelings to the surface. Grief can also feel like failure: my life is not working out as planned, this tragedy was not in my script. There can even be a superstitious fear that I must have done something wrong, or my friends must think I have done something wrong, because the sun is not shining on me as was once expected. Jesus flatly refused to make this link when pressed to do so. All the great men and women of the Bible went through very dark times. Including Jesus. Those who love strongly, grieve deeply.

Jesus knows what it is to have love rejected. He weeps over Jerusalem, weeping over the missed opportunities when people choose not to receive the love that is offered. Jesus knows how much it hurts when love is ignored, mocked or spurned.

He knows what it is to be betrayed. We do not fully know why Judas turned traitor, this disciple who had heard so many of Jesus' words and who had seen so many extraordinary events. It may have been about money or misplaced expectations or some motive lost to history. And then Peter denies he knows Jesus at all. When we are deeply let down by friends, Jesus knows what that feels like.

And he knows what it is to mourn the loss of a friend. The grief for the one is an echo of the grief for the many; when Jesus wept at the tomb of Lazarus he not only had in mind one person and one family, he was weighed down by the sorrow and pain of the continued presence of death in the world and all the suffering that this brings.

People rightly talk about the problem of suffering but it is only a philosophical or intellectual problem (rather than an emotional or practical one) if we believe that this was not how the world was meant to be. And because it was not meant to be like this, Jesus weeps at a funeral. And goes on to do something somewhat bigger, but that is for a later reading. For the moment let us hold on to the belief that we can trust that Jesus grieves with those who grieve. He never takes it lightly.

Reflection 15

Day 6   To know what it is to be alone
Matthew 26:36-46

In the garden of Gethsemane his friends could not stay awake. Despite their close proximity Jesus felt profoundly alone. Perhaps there was an echo of the loneliness of the time three years earlier in the desert after his baptism and before his public ministry began. He goes to Gethsemane between the last supper and the world's new chapter that his crucifixion the next day will usher in. In Gethsemane he is in the wilderness once more.

Solitude, being apart from the busyness of social interaction, can be very positive. It provides opportunities for reflection and prayer, for dancing to a slower rhythm. Jesus made time to do this.

Loneliness, when we feel left out of a group, no longer part of the circle and unsure where friends are to be found, is a difficult journey to travel. Jesus knows this feeling, too.

Jesus knows what it means to go through the barren times, those seasons when we feel we achieve nothing, seasons when it appears that others are detached from what is happening inside of us. These are challenging times, and we are sometimes tempted to avoid the wilderness at all costs, but in the Bible narratives desert experiences are seen as very significant. The being away from, the being outside of, the normal is often a time of deep growth.

Sometimes we choose to go, sometimes we are pushed into it: whatever the reason for the time in the wilderness it is good to remember that Jesus has been there, and that his pathway through was to stay obedient, to remember who he was and to confirm his calling.

There can be a danger in solitude; it can become self-indulgent and self-centred with no regard for seeing it as a resource which can help us serve others better. There can be a danger in loneliness; it can lead to self-pity, the desire inappropriately to force relationships to happen or the need for constant reassurance.

Whether it is about solitude or loneliness we can remember that the wilderness season does not last for ever. The new chapter begins and, changed and invigorated, we can face it afresh. We need not be frightened of being alone. It was part of Jesus' story and he used these times well.

Reflection 16

Day 7 . . . . *To know what it
is to be tempted
Matthew 4:1-11
Hebrews 4:15*

In the wilderness Jesus was tempted. Tempted to satisfy his needs and desires by the wrong route, tempted to look impressive and tempted to force God's hand. These temptations were explicitly focused on identity and can be summarised as: "If you are the Son of God, then surely this would be an appropriate/shrewd/clever way to behave." The question lying behind all temptations lies behind his: What does it mean to be you?

He is able to resist temptation by being secure in his relationship with God and by understanding what the Bible says. He does not try and meet his needs by using the wrong methods (turning stone into bread). He does not look to a different authority than God himself (worshipping, investing in, all that the subtle powers of evil have to offer). He will not carry out his mission by using inappropriate spectacular means (throwing himself from the temple). Through them all, he uses the Bible in his responses. His adversary uses the Bible, too, but Jesus understands the context of the passages he is quoting. He is reading it with humility, the adversary is reading it to exploit it for his own purposes.

The writer of the letter to the Hebrews says that Jesus knows what it is to be tempted. This is comforting because resisting temptation can feel a lonely struggle; it is encouraging because it reminds us that the temptation does not have to win. Sometimes we give up rather too quickly, or tell ourselves that we lack the energy to go on resisting. The temptation can seem to have the biggest voice in our life at the moment. Jesus has the stronger voice.

In listening to that stronger voice we get things back in perspective. It tells us that we really do not need to do 'this' to make us happy, in fact, 'this' is very likely to cause unhappiness to others and ourselves.

The temptations that Jesus faced in the wilderness, and the underlying identity question, are common to us all. We will not explicitly articulate it but we might often be thinking: "Because I am me, and my future or needs or tiredness or background are so special and so unique, surely it is entirely right for me to do this (even though I would rush to condemn it in someone else)".

Jesus knows the subtle pressures of temptations in wilderness times but he also knows they can be resisted. It is never a failure to be tempted, but it is a failure to embrace and indulge the temptation, to choose to welcome it as a friend instead of showing it the door.

These thoughts are meant to encourage us, not lead us to despair about past or present failings. As we shall see, when we do fall to temptation there is forgiveness on offer. There is always time for a new beginning.

Reflection 17

Day 8 . . . . . . To enjoy a party
John 2:1-14

Jesus and his friends were invited to a wedding party. There is no evidence that they were close relatives, so perhaps they were invited simply because the couple wanted them there. Perhaps they are fun to have at a wedding. Perhaps it would feel rather special to have Jesus present. Whatever the reason, it seems likely that they knew that Jesus would not ruin things, otherwise he would not have been invited. They were right, Jesus goes to considerable lengths to keep the party going. Water is turned into wine, the ordinary to special, the party is renewed. This is later recorded by John as being the first 'sign' of who Jesus is. Not something religious done in the temple, not a great spectacle of thunder and lightning on a holy mountain, not a dramatic speech to thousands, but helping out at a party so that a young wedding couple would not be socially embarrassed in Cana of Galilee.

And this party attitude led to constant complaints about Jesus by those who had rather fixed views of what it meant to be Godly. They were doing all they could to keep themselves undefiled. He was eating and drinking with 'sinful' people and then had the audacity to say that those who did not feel themselves to be sinful were not invited to his party.

The father in Jesus' story of the returning child not only throws a party for the errant younger son, but then makes a particular effort to bring the grumpy older brother into the jollity. Lovers of Dickens may recall that the young Scrooge could not understand the generosity of Mr Fezziwig. How we respond when others rejoice is revealing.

The bread and wine of Communion mean so many things, among them is a reminder that there is celebration in heaven. The great priest poet George Herbert in the 17th century pondered whether the best way to receive the bread and wine of Communion was to be sitting, as a reminder that this is a feast. If we trust in Jesus we are responding to an invitation to a party.

Some of us like noisy parties, some of us like quieter affairs. It is not so much the *type* of party that Jesus affirms, it is more the understanding that celebrations, friendships and joy deeply matter. When we smile or sing or dance for joy, whether quietly or exuberantly, then Jesus is there at the feast with us.

Reflection 18

Day 9 . . . . . *To care for the*
strangest sort of people
Luke 19:1-10

Jesus was on the road to Jerusalem. His journey
takes him through Jericho and the crowds are out
to meet him. Jesus makes a point of picking out
one of the least popular men in the town, a traitor
(he was working for the occupying Romans) and
a cheat (he had used his rank as a tax-collector to
extort more than he should from his neighbours).
He had been watching Jesus from a tree, too short
to see over the crowd on ground level and perhaps
not wanting to get close to others.

Jesus greets the man by name and gives him the
honour of going to his home. The crowd mutters
about Jesus' lack of discernment. Does he not know
what this looks like? Does he just do it to annoy?
But Zacchaeus then emerges and announces that
this meeting has changed him. He publicly admits
his fraudulent ways and promises to make good.
Jesus then calmly assumes the right to use Godly
words of restoration: "Today salvation has come

to this house, because this man, too, is a son of Abraham." And reminds the crowd of his mission: "For the Son of Man came to seek and to save what was lost."

Did Zacchaeus really want to be included? Perhaps he had simply gone up the tree to look from a distance. This is the risky part of being open-minded with Jesus, you never know where a secretive glance may lead. A conversation with a friend, a visit to a sacred place, a glimpse of a magazine article, a walk across a mountain and suddenly your heart and mind are being stirred up and you sense the invitation to take a step further.

We are told that Zacchaeus "welcomed him gladly"– perhaps there was some slight something in him that was already pleased that Jesus was passing through his town. Perhaps here was a person who would not exclude and despise him, someone who might give him some attention and interest, someone who might even understand why he had taken that compromising and unpopular job as a tax collector in the first place.

Whatever Zacchaeus' original motives were, it was a lesson clearly proclaimed to everyone present: This Jesus is willing to engage with anyone, even a tax-collector who made his money by paying the hated Romans and pressing down hard on the long suffering Jericho citizens.

The birth of the saviour was proclaimed by the angels as good news to the whole world. Jesus came to seek the lost, every one of them. If you are one in a hundred sheep and you are the one that goes missing, you are the one he wants to find, you are the one he wants to lead safely home. You are loved and valued beyond measure. So is your neighbour.

Reflection 19

Day 10 .   To include the inarticulate
Matthew 19:13-15

He also included children.

Some parents brought children to Jesus; his followers shooed them away, trying to stop them from getting too close. Jesus says firmly, "Let the little children come to me, and do not hinder them, for the kingdom of heaven belongs to such as these."

We do not know why the disciples were so protective. Perhaps they thought Jesus was not good with children and it would all be rather awkward, or that the toddlers would make a noise or that they had no place in the deep purposes of God. Whatever the reason, they got it badly wrong. And it was such an important mistake that they were publicly corrected and they then wanted their error to be recorded in the stories that circulated around Jesus, presumably so that the later followers would learn the lesson.

This incident immediately raises questions for those who see the expression of faith only as a cerebral exercise. If little children, who cannot articulate very well, who may not quite behave as we wish and who are rather good at being undignified, are part of Jesus' welcome, then this welcome may be wider, and may work in different ways, than we think. If a relationship with God is fully available to little children then we can assume it is equally available to all those whom we may consider to be inarticulate, unable to behave 'properly' or who are undignified.

And it can be of some comfort and encouragement for those of us who wonder if dementia may strike. Our relationship with God will remain intact. Christianity believes in a God who is big enough not to have his relationship limited and narrowed by an individual's mental ability.

Jesus is making a direct point about inclusivity and welfare of children, as well as the value of simple faith. It therefore includes a challenge to ensure children are protected in our society. We are entrusted to protect children against harm and this includes guarding them against such destructive enemies as racism, greed, sexualisation, violence, sexism, or selfish ambition. Winston Churchill once said that the best investment a society can make is to feed children. Jesus calls us to be as careful to give them good emotional food as we are to give them healthy physical food.

Is it more important to encourage a child to grow up to be a good person, to pass all their exams with top grades or to win a talent show? Yes, some can do all three, but which ultimately is most important?

We remember that once on a hillside Jesus accepted the gift of bread and fish from a child. There must have been something about Jesus, and what he was saying, that meant he was of interest to young people. The child had come to hear him speak and he felt included. His gifts were received and blessed, and were multiplied for the good of others.

Reflection 20

Day 11 . . . . To endow our gifts
with eternal value
John 6:1-13
Romans 12:3-8

Were people smirking patronisingly as the bread and fish were taken to Jesus? It was not very much, offered by a child who clearly had no understanding of what was needed. Not that we were doing very much to help, it must be said, but at least we were not looking a little foolish by pretending we could do something. Perhaps others joined us in laughing at the child's fish and bread being brought to the front of the huge crowd.

Jesus does not laugh.

He takes the offering, gives thanks and feeds the multitudes. He accepts the gift. He does not mock or turn away. The child offers and the miracle happens.

If there is something that we are able to offer to serve God and neighbour, then let us offer it. The boy did not keep his sandwiches hidden in his pocket for fear others would laugh. He did not keep them all to himself, hoping to eat them when no one else was looking. He did not play the game selfishly or safely. He offered what he had.

If we find it difficult to offer our gifts, it is worth examining our feelings and our motives. Sometimes it is fear that keeps people from being the "cheerful giver" that Paul commends – perhaps fear that once something has been given it will be lost; perhaps fear that the gift will be rejected. Or maybe, tragically, no one has ever told us that we have gifts to contribute. We cannot see our own role in the play. Even if someone tells us we are on stage, script in hand, we assume this is a case of mistaken identity and it is not really our lines that are required.

Paul writes about how our gifts match with those offered by others. It is as if we each bring a piece to the jig-saw, the picture is incomplete without it. We are the body of Christ, every limb and organ is needed. We each need the wisdom in equal measure to honour our gifts and those brought by others. If we see someone offering their gifts, however inadequate or irrelevant they may seem to be, then it is holy to encourage, guide and support them. We are on dangerous ground if we do not.

Reflection 21

Day 12   To know that we like to learn
Matthew, chapters 5-7

There he was, walking around, chatting, a greeting here and a smile there - and then he sits down. Quiet spreads through the crowd because the sitting down means he is going to teach. It is electrifying, people really want to hear what he is going to say. And he seems to think that they need to hear it.

The effectiveness of a teacher is partly dependent on the student. Are we willing to be taught? Jesus taught about love, anxiety, priorities, faith, justice, integrity, humility mercy and relationships. He talked about the dangers of setting our hearts on the treasures of this world. He taught about prayer and giving, and what it meant to be part of the community he was leading, to be subjects in the kingdom he was proclaiming. He taught about God, reconciliation and accountability. He used humour, stories, actions and instruction.

If we wish to learn from him, we may need to unlearn some teachings we have learnt from elsewhere. If we have been brought up to think we can achieve all we want in our own strength, or that desire for money and comfort should drive our ambitions, or that it is acceptable to put down others or lie about them to get our own way, then we will need to unlearn these lessons. We may have got very used to them, they may have been taught to us, or modelled to us, by loved and respected people. We may be scared of seeing things differently, and the change of teacher may feel difficult.

Reflecting upon, and obeying, the teachings of Jesus is a sign that we trust that he knows best. We may not feel like being generous to someone, but we trust that this is the right thing for us as well as them. We may want to allow our worry to grow and build until it is the largest emotion we hold but Jesus tells us to take things one day at a time. We may find it easier to follow the fashions and values of this world but we trust that Jesus knows better than the voices of current culture.

The teachings of Jesus, and indeed of some of the leaders of the early church, are not always easy to follow. We will have to use our own minds and the wisdom of others. Peter commented that some of Paul's writings were difficult to understand, but it did not stop him commending them to his readers, and indeed putting them on the same level as 'The Scriptures'. Thus we need help: if we only read the teachings of Jesus and the early church by ourselves or with people just like us we are likely to impose our own views and values on them. G. K. Chesterton has his detective Father Brown comment: "When will people understand that it is useless for a man to read his Bible unless he also reads everyone else's Bible?" When we remember that we are part of a much wider community, one that values hearing the thoughts of others, we are more likely to sit humbly under the truths we read.

People liked listening to Jesus. At one time the crowd on the hillside was at least five thousand, they were willing to sit and listen and did not really notice when mealtimes passed by. At the very least, Jesus must have been *interesting* to hear. As we study his words it is helpful to ask "What is *interesting* in this? What should be grabbing my attention and making me think?"

Reflection 22

Day 13 . . . . . To be thankful
1 Corinthians 11:23-26

On the night before he died, knowing all that was to come, and all that this meal of bread and wine was going to come to mean and to signify, Jesus thanked God. If ever there were a moment when it would have been understandable not to feel thankful, this would be it. But he did not simply hold the bread, soon to be broken, and accept it in words of resignation. He gave thanks for it.

It is sometimes very difficult to be thankful, especially if there seems to be nothing good going on. To be thankful one has to be able to see the bigger picture, and in the midst of the darkness that can be very hard to do.

Sometimes darkness comes and there seems to be no light. Sometimes we cannot see any reason to be thankful and it is a sign of deep trust in a person to be thankful when there is no obvious reason to be so. There is strength and comfort in remembering that there is something here, somehow, somewhere, for which we can be thankful. Perhaps it is the depth of love that is now being expressed in grief. Perhaps it is a bird singing. Perhaps it is the courage to take one more step, even though there seems no reason to do so. Perhaps it is simply that we are us, and deeply loved and honoured even while the immediate weather is so bleak.

Corrie Ten Boom tells of her shock when her sister thanked God for the fleas in their beds in their concentration camp barracks. It was only later that they discovered that these fleas had kept the guards away and thus their extraordinary ministry of comfort and teaching had continued undisturbed.

What is there in this situation that Jesus would be thankful for in the middle of all the current mess and sadness? We can ask the same question when everything seems to be going marvellously well. What is it in this situation that is good and honourable? To be thankful, not smug, in the good times; to be thankful, not despairing, in the bad.

In that moment of imminent betrayal, suffering and death, Jesus thanked God for the bread. On a hillside being watched by thousands, when offered a gift by a child, Jesus thanked God for the bread.

When we are thankful we are showing humility because we are acknowledging our need of others and our appreciation of their gifts. When we trust Jesus, we can trust him to be thankful for us and for what we offer; we can trust him to find something worth being thankful for.

Reflection 23

Day 14 .   .   .   .   To forgive
Luke 5:17-26
Romans 8:31-39

The friends must have been rather deflated to see such a crowd around the house, guessing that the inside was already packed. Their determination is not to be thwarted and they manage to clamber up on to the roof, half-dragging, half-pulling, their paralysed friend with them. They open up the roof and lower him down to the healer.

"Friend, your sins are forgiven."

The friends, peering down through the roof, are somewhat surprised. But it is the religious leaders and the legal intelligentsia who speak first. They hear these words and wonder what was going on, "Who is this fellow who speaks blasphemy? Who can forgive sins but God alone?"

Jesus knows what is flashing across their minds and searchingly asks, "Why are you thinking these things in your hearts?"

Because, they want to splutter, what you have just said, carpenter's son, is completely out of order. You are claiming the right to forgive the sins of this man you have never met before. You are claiming to do what we all know only God can do, that is, to forgive sins. That is why we are thinking these things. And if we are honest, we are now feeling a mix of things. Some of us are glad because you have delivered yourself into our hands, we've got you now. Some are completely shocked. And some, very secretly, are quietly but excitedly wondering if there might be more to you than meets the eye.

"Which is easier:" continues Jesus, "to say, 'Your sins are forgiven,' or to say, 'Get up and walk'? But that you may know that the Son of Man has authority on earth to forgive sins…" He turns to the paralysed man: "I tell you, get up, take your mat and go home."

Jesus forgives. He sees it as more important than the physical healing which was done almost as an afterthought, just to drive the point home (although we suspect Jesus knew all along that the man would leave on his own two feet).

Reflection 24

Day 15 . . To insist that sin matters
Romans 6:23
2 Corinthians 5:17-19

Jesus forgives. Yesterday, dear reader, you deliberately did something that you knew was wrong. Sorry if that offends you, but that is the way it is. If it is any comfort, so did I. Probably much worse than your misdemeanour. We can provide all manner of excuses – we were tired, he is so irritating, everyone else does it, it was just once - but at the heart we made an inner decision to do the wrong thing. We missed the mark of our own standards, let alone God's. This is sin, and we cannot read the New Testament without noticing that Jesus takes it seriously. If Jesus did not think anyone sinned, he would not have needed to talk about forgiveness. If Jesus did not think it was important, he would have healed the paralytic first and left the forgiveness for another time. If Jesus did not think sin mattered, he would not have come to die.

We are not to despair over our sins. If we do so, we are forgetting that that Jesus *can* forgive and that he *wants* to forgive. But it may be necessary to be reminded why it is helpful to think seriously about it. Sin spoils relationships and our own sense of self-worth. It is habit-forming and destructive. The dirt mounts up, covering the true self, full of glorious potential, with layers of deceit or pride or selfishness. It promises happiness and delivers shame, it can lead to a craving for more when the first (or fifteenth) attempt at satisfaction turns out to be a failure. Chesterton's Father Brown remarks: "Men may keep a sort of level of good, but no man has ever been able to keep on one level of evil. That road goes down and down." The road goes down and down. One lie leads to another. Gossip leads to contempt. Envy leads to hate.

Sin is serious. As the old saying has it, sin separates, spoils and spreads. Anything that is taken seriously needs a serious response. To forgive, clean up and restore, is always costly. There is always sacrifice in the healing, and sometimes the sacrifice needs to be very deep indeed.

John Newton, whose career as a slave-trader provided a particular insight into the seriousness of sin, said just before he died: "Although my memory's fading, I remember two things very clearly: I am a great sinner and Christ is a great Saviour."

Reflection 25

Day 16 . . . . To die for us
1 Peter 2:24

We can trust Jesus to love us enough to die for us. As simple as that. No easy way of saying it.

Crucifixion was a bloody, horrific and certain way to die, which is why the Romans used it so often to punish criminals or rebels. In becoming like us Jesus had already sacrificially divested himself of more than we can ever grasp. On that Friday afternoon, as he hung on the cross, he was a victim of the injustice, hate and fear and greed that was part of the world then and is equally such a sad part of it today. The trial and crucifixion would have been seen by the authorities as a messy but quite successful outcome of some necessary manipulation. But his followers very quickly came to see the crucifixion as more than yet another example of the abuse of power. Peter was to write: "He himself bore our sins in his body on the tree, so that we might die to sins and live for righteousness; by his wounds you have been healed."

He sacrificed himself in our place, so that the guilt and shame, the dirt and separation of sin, could be soaked up, taken care of, in his death. And what happened two days later would show he had the power to do it.

It is deeply moving when we discover that someone has willingly sacrificed something for our sake. It may seem a small matter, perhaps they laid down their desire to go to the cinema so you could go bowling. Or it may be larger, a career is calmly paused or ended so you can be looked after or so you can pursue a dream. Good parents sacrifice deeply for their children. Good partners sacrifice deeply for each other. Each sacrifice we make for someone else is a tiny, or less than tiny, kind of death. Christians believe that Jesus sacrificed himself for you and for me. If ever you are not sure you are loved, look at a cross and remember that he did that for you.

What happened when Jesus was crucified was of eternal significance. And it was done out of love. He died for you, not to add cold statistics of the numbers of those who are forgiven, but because he particularly likes your company and does not want anything to get in the way of your relationship with God. You can trust him to love you enough to die for you.

The joy and liberation of forgiveness means that Paul is later able to write to the Christians in Rome "If God is for us, who can be against us? He who did not spare his own Son, but gave him up for us all—how will he not also, along with him, graciously give us all things? Who will bring any charge against those whom God has chosen? It is God who justifies. Who then can condemn? Christ Jesus who died - more than that, who was raised to life - is at the right hand of God and is also interceding for us." And to those in Corinth: "God was reconciling the world to himself in Christ, not counting people's sins against them." And this is just after he has reminded his readers "Therefore, if anyone is in Christ, there is a new creation: The old has gone, the new has come!" Jesus restores, renews and reconciles.

It is all rather exciting.

Reflection 26

Day 17 .   .   .   .   To conquer death
(the walls are coming down)
John 14:1-6 1
Corinthians 15:12-20

Crucifixion was effective and permanent; no one comes back from that. But then, it is claimed, he did.

Jesus had promised that death would not be able to hold him and that he has the power to take us through death to heaven. Death is always profound and often unspeakably sad. If it is not the end after all, if it is a comma, not a full stop, then vital hope is added to the mix of grief and memories and a whole new perspective is brought to bear on our lives on earth. Perhaps, as glimpsed and guessed in virtually every tribe and culture and faith across the world, there is indeed more to life than this.

The elephant in the room, the unspoken large truth that we do not often consider, is that one day we will die. As soon as we know that we are facing death sooner than we thought we would, or as soon as we know of the terminal illness or sudden death of a friend or family member, then we remember the significance of the fact of death. We can trust Jesus to take us through even this.

The night before he died, Jesus said these words: "Do not let your hearts be troubled. Trust in God; trust also in me. In my Father's house are many rooms; if it were not so, I would have told you. I am going there to prepare a place for you. And if I go and prepare a place for you, I will come back and take you to be with me that you also may be where I am."

We may continue to be frightened of the process of dying, which can be distressing and painful. Jesus wept at the tomb of Lazarus and in Gethsemane at the thought of it all. We can be frightened of how others may cope without us. There is much that rightly may make us anxious, but we do not need to be frightened of death itself. On the Sunday after the Friday, Jesus was alive. Edwin's advisor was struck that Paulinus was talking about someone who claimed to know what happens outside the hall of our earthly life *(see page 32)*. The claim of resurrection puts Jesus into a different league.

And the outside that the sparrow flies towards is not as cold and wintry as Edwin was told. It is a feast and a celebration, more satisfying and complete than the hall itself.

If there is a heaven then there is a wider reality that we can only now glimpse or imagine. But we can trust that all that is truly good this side of death is an echo of a greater good that one day we will share. C. S. Lewis has Jewel say in 'The Last Battle.': "I have come home at last! This is my real country! I belong here. This is the land I have been looking for all my life, though I never knew it till now... Come further up, come further in!"

The walls of Edwin's hall have come down. Jesus can be trusted to take us through death. And one last thing: the risen Jesus made time to meet with one grumpy doubter who had refused the invitation to be with his friends the week before. Risen in glory but still caring for the individual. And it worked.

Reflection 27

Day 18 . . . . . To pray for us
Mark 1:35
John 17:20
Hebrews 7:24,25

Yesterday's focus should not have surprised us. Nearly all of my previous reflections have presupposed that Jesus continues to be active and dynamic. If he truly continues to be welcoming, forgiving, teaching, affirming and so on, this is only possible if he is alive. Today and tomorrow we will look at two further things that we can trust him to do, as much now as when he was in Galilee or Jerusalem.

We can trust him to pray. The praying is inextricably part of Jesus' ministry of reconciliation and restoration. The writer of the letter to the Hebrews says "Because Jesus lives for ever he has a permanent priesthood. Therefore he is able to save completely those who come to God through him, because he always lives to intercede for them."

Louis Berkhof writes:

> *It is a consoling thought that Christ is praying
> for us, even when we are negligent in our
> prayer life; that he is presenting to the Father
> those spiritual needs which were not present
> to our minds and which we often neglect to
> include in our prayers; and that He prays for
> our protection against the dangers of which we
> are not even conscious, and against the enemies
> which threaten us, though we do not notice it.
> He is praying that our faith may not cease, and
> that we may come out victoriously in the end.*
> *(Systematic Theology, p.403)*

In Jesus' earthly ministry it was sometimes frustrating for his friends: people thought they knew where Jesus was, only to find out he had slipped away to be on his own and to pray. He prayed, and he included us in his prayers. "My prayer is not for them alone," he said, referring to his immediate followers. "I pray also for those who believe in me through their message." And that refers to people like you and me.

After healing many, Jesus went out early in the morning to pray. Later, before he chose the apostles, he prayed. Jesus prayed for Peter before Peter himself knew he was going to be tempted to deny his friend and teacher. While being crucified, he was praying for those who had put him on the cross.

We can trust Jesus to be praying for us. As the hymn writer William Chatterton Dix has it:

Intercessor, friend of sinners,
earth's redeemer plead for me.

And he does. Whatever else is happening in our lives today, we are being held in the prayers of Jesus.

Reflection 28

Day 19   To Judge with perfect justice
             Matthew 25:31-46

We are asked to trust in a Jesus who claims he has the ultimate right to comment on our behaviour, thoughts and attitudes. Alongside the authoritative teaching style and the claim to have power to forgive sins, the calm statement that it would be him that would judge the world caused quite a stir.

Our choice of 'voice' to be our judge is always revealing. "What would my boss think? What would my parents think? What would that particular group of friends think?" are all valid questions, but it is important to consider who has the most important voice in our lives. Christianity holds that "What would Jesus think?" is the ultimate reference point, however worthy and helpful the other voices may be.

Jesus not only assumed the right to speak about the present, he claimed that he would one day bring all things to a close and that his judgement in those last days would be the one that mattered. In the startling parable of the sheep and the goats, we note that not only it is the "Son of Man" (one of his titles) who will judge, but that it is this same Son of Man who is the ongoing reference point for our actions. If I offer someone a drink, I am offering Jesus a drink. If I withhold compassion from a friend or stranger, then I am withholding compassion from Jesus. Jesus will call me to account for my attitudes and actions in these matters. Jesus is rather more interested in this than he is in the colour of my new kitchen or the size of my pension plan.

My judgements are often wrong. I misread situations and people. I misunderstand words that are spoken. I misunderstand what is being thought behind the words. I do not fully grasp people's motives. (Maybe they do not fully know their own motives, either. I certainly get confused about mine. I am as poor a judge about myself and my actions as I may be about anyone else.) If Jesus is the judge who matters, then I can sit more lightly on my own opinions about others and myself.

Sometimes in Victorian homes there were plaques reminding households that "God is watching". In our day we take down the plaques. Two thousand years ago we crucified. Anything to pretend that we need not be concerned with what he thinks.

Part of the judgement of Jesus was that he could spot hypocrites and he spoke strongly to them. It is possible that others who were listening did not know these people were hypocrites until Jesus spoke these words (a defining feature of hypocrisy is that it wants to be hidden). If we deliberately keep our outside different from our inside (and in this internet age people may have several 'outside' profiles), if we pretend that we are better than we are so that others will feel worse about themselves, then we do well to be aware of the searching eyes of Christ.

But we are to be reassured, we are asked to trust that judgement is in the hands of Jesus, who is full of understanding, wisdom and mercy. Who else would we rather have?

Reflection 29

Day 20   To show us what God is like
John 14:1-6,
Colossians 1:15-19

The most controversial and overarching claim is this and it includes all the previous promises we have touched on: we can trust Jesus to show us what God is like.

Jesus was brought to Pilate to be tried because "He claimed to be the Son of God." His words and actions over the previous three years had led many to say that he was claiming to be divine. When he arrived in Jerusalem on Palm Sunday the authorities were not only scared that the Romans would react angrily to the arrival of a king-like figure in the middle of the crowded festival of Passover, they were already understandably offended by his claim to be God-like. Did he really say he was the good shepherd? Surely only "The Lord is my shepherd". Did he claim he could forgive sins? That was what God does. Did he echo the personal title of God when he said "Before Abraham was born, *I AM?*"

The Roman emperors used to style themselves as divine, but that was not taken very seriously. It was taken very seriously indeed in the case of Jesus, by his enemies as well as his supporters. The religious leaders were shocked and offended. He was disruptive, offensive and blasphemous. And so he was killed.

On the night before he died Jesus said to Philip "Anyone who has seen me has seen the Father. How can you say 'Show us the Father?' Don't you believe that I am in the Father and the Father is in me?" We note the enormity of this claim. If our neighbour, colleague or a political leader said: "Anyone who has seen me has seen God," we would be concerned for their sanity.

About thirty years later Paul wrote about Jesus in his letter to the Colossians "He is the image of the invisible God, the firstborn over all creation. For by him all things were created: things in heaven and on earth, visible and invisible, whether thrones or powers or rulers or authorities; all things were created by him and for him. He is before all things, and in him all things hold together... For God was pleased to have all his fullness dwell in him." That is an extraordinary paragraph. Jesus was a poor and localised figure in a small province in the Roman Empire, and yet Paul wrote these words about him.

Most people around the world and through history say that they believe in some sort of God. But what sort of God do they and we mean? The God may be a result of fears, desires, upbringing and false thinking. We may end up worshipping a distant and terrifying creation of our misunderstandings, perhaps an oppressive figure who spends his time longing to catch us out, thinks lowly of us, and never smiles. Or our God can be the image of us. Thinking as we do, approving our ideas, and wholeheartedly agreeing with every judgement we make. This is the easiest sort of God to worship.

Or our God can be a sort of sanctified Father Christmas, doling out the good things, avoiding the difficult questions, and only turning up very occasionally. Or perhaps God reduces to some vague expression of the beauty of nature.

If Jesus truly showed us what God is like, then these other images will simply be idols, created by us. They will have to go. This is at the heart of all these narratives and letters: if we want to know what God is like, look at Jesus.

Reflection 30

Day 21 . . . . To make us think
John 20:24-31

The moment of recognition – "My Lord and my God" – was transformative. A moment of brightest clarity and deepest assurance. And the fact it was the blunt and cautious doubter who said it perhaps meant it carried even greater power. If even *he* sees it now, the others may have murmured, then who knows what other lives may be changed? This all might get to be quite big…

We are told that if we wonder what God is really like, then we are to look at Jesus. And all the other idols will have to be put to one side. We will learn something of the compassion, authority and mercy of God. We will learn that he likes us to use our minds and does not always give straightforward answers. He likes telling stories and he likes forgiving people. We will learn that he will talk with anyone who is interested and that there are no 'outcasts' to him. We will learn that he can get angry at hypocrisy and those who lay unnecessary burdens on others. (It is no wonder that the Bible has been a source of terror to despots across history. What might the downtrodden people do if they learn that the God they worship really is interested in them?) We will learn that this is a God whose love can be rejected. We will learn that this is a God who knows what it is to suffer. We will learn that God is bigger than death and can lead us safely through it. We will learn that he values love, honesty and humility and says rather uncomfortable things about money.

We can no longer hide behind our imaginings. We are no longer making a God to order. How would we have felt walking with Jesus in AD 30? Would we have been some of those who are muttering behind our hands that Jesus is spending time with outcasts? Would we, as the disciples sometimes tried to do, have attempted to write Jesus' script for him? If so, perhaps we have a tendency to tell God what he should be doing (which tends to be what we think would suit us best) and this is always going to end up looking rather silly.

Jesus was interested in people, engaging with them, challenging them and welcoming them. This is what God is like. It is encouraging and liberating because we can begin to have a sense of what is expected of us. If we offer a cup of water to the thirsty then we know that God is smiling. If, like the child on the hillside with the five thousand, we bring our gifts, however small they may seem to us, then he will multiply them and bless others with them. If we ever find ourselves asking for help, we are very much on the right lines. We are free to lose that destructive competitiveness that leads us to use our strength to crush, not build up. Now we have a guide who can release us to consider life's true meaning.

Reflection 31

Day 22 .   .   Does he trust us, does he
takes us seriously?
Acts 1:1-8

Jesus said these words to the disciples as they wondered how they would continue without him:

> *You will receive power when the Holy Spirit*
> *comes on you; and you will be my witnesses in*
> *Jerusalem, and in all Judea and Samaria, and*
> *to the ends of the earth.*

The power is given so that Jesus will be honoured in our lives. Our behaviour and words are to speak of his nature and values. Jesus told his followers that they would be his witnesses to their own circle in Jerusalem, then to the surrounding area, including those despised Samaritans, and then to the whole world.

Some people, sadly, have been made to think that they are not to be taken seriously, that they have no real value, that their voices do not matter, that they have no place at the table and there is little they can contribute. And now here is someone who says that their voices do count, that they are welcome at the table and that their actions profoundly matter.

It is a wonderful calling: we are to be witnesses throughout the world to the love of God. We cannot do this in our own strength, hence Jesus' reference to the Holy Spirit. We have to be on our guard against anything that might prevent us receiving this divine help. Perhaps we have become proud and feel we no longer have any need of God. Or perhaps we are close to absolute despair and feel we cannot move. Perhaps we are fearful of the inevitable change as God challenges and empowers us to look outwards and onwards; it may feel much better and safer to keep things as they are. Or perhaps there is a favourite sin that deep down we do not want to lose and we know that if we are serious about following Jesus then that will come under the spotlight.

And so we need to be reminded that God has great things in store for us. There will be tasks of love and compassion, growth in holiness, relationships, understanding and faith. Paul told the Ephesians that they are "God's handiwork, created in Christ Jesus to do good works." What may be these "good works" be for us today? We cannot be entirely sure until we get there, but they are likely to include something of love, commitment and integrity. There will be something about using our gifts positively and about bringing encouragement to others. God's Holy Spirit, promised to us by Jesus, brings gifts and makes us fruitful so that the great works can continue. We are trusted to get on with it. He takes us seriously and has high expectations. We are called to change the world.

Reflection 32

Day 23 . . .   *But he does not force*
                               Mark 10:17-21

The conversation had been going so well. This committed, clean-living, religious young man is talking with Jesus. He, the disciples whisper to each other, is said to be rather wealthy. Always useful for a fledgling movement whose leader seems rather uninterested in worldly comforts. Perhaps this new convert will sponsor some donkeys. At least that would save all this walking around.

But then the mood changes. Jesus has put his finger on something that the young man finds it difficult to give up. (As an aside, we note that some would have said "Sell everything you have and give the money to us", Jesus says "Sell everything you have and give to the poor." He is infuriatingly uncommitted to the idea of those new smart donkeys.)

Jesus assures him that the young man's sacrifice and generosity will be richly appreciated and rewarded and looks at him "and loved him". This is about welcome and invitation, not condemnation. But we read that "The man's face fell. He went away sad, because he had great wealth."

Jesus wants the best for us. Not the fairly ordinary, but the best. And so he continues to help us to grow, whether by questions, challenges, affirmation or comfort. He wants us to face ourselves as we are and glimpse the potential of what we might be. "Do you want to get well?" he asked a crippled man (and crippling can happen in all sorts of ways). The answer is often more complex than we expect, which is why the question is always worth asking. We sometimes want to stay where we are, even when that place is not healthy. It is our way of coping, it is familiar and accustomed and anything else feels frightening.

The love of God is offered unconditionally. But, like all love, it can only be received if it is, well, received. Jesus did not say that this receiving would always be easy. If we are determined to keep our hearts, minds and ambitions full of other things, we might not wish to receive his transforming love. In Holman Hunt's much-loved picture of Jesus knocking on the door of our hearts, based on the Bible verse Revelation 3:20, "Here I am! I stand at the door and knock. If anyone hears my voice and opens the door, I will come in and eat with them, and they with me", there is no handle on the outside of the door. We have the freedom to keep the door closed. Love does not force.

And he will respect the choice that we have made. If we deliberately, informedly, continually, reject the invitation to love the needy, if we constantly choose to reject whatever we understand of the gracious love and forgiveness of God then that rejection will be sadly accepted. And so in Jesus' parable about sheep and goats the choices made by the unkind are acknowledged. They want nothing to do with the overflowing love of God and their wishes ultimately will be honoured. The story of the person burying his talents has a similar theme: don't be the one that hides what you have been given and then deliberately use false reasoning to justify your selfishness.

Deep down most of us like to trust someone who respects us enough that our response matters. But it can be uncomfortable to be taken so seriously.

Reflection 33

Day 24 . . .   A call to be humble,
*   just and merciful*
*   Luke 18:9-14*
*   Micah 6:8*

If he takes us seriously, what does he expect us to do?

Jesus told a story of two men in a temple. He needed to warn his listeners, especially the ones who felt they had all the answers and all the behavioural boxes ticked, to beware of having confidence in their own goodness and to stop looking down on everyone else. In the story the tax-collector was in a right relationship with God because he knew he was a sinner, was humble, and asked for help. The self-sufficient and self-satisfied character was the one who got it wrong.

It is difficult for the worldly-successful and worldly-wise to admit they might need something or someone bigger than themselves. But being prepared to accept that we are sometimes in need of help is seen as a sign of strength, peace and wisdom. It is liberating to know that we are part of a mutually giving and receiving community. It is likewise liberating to know our need of God.

The words of the prophet Micah, probably written about eight hundred years earlier, would have been known by everyone in Jesus' circle.

And what does the Lord require of you?
To act justly and to love mercy
and to walk humbly with your God.

Throughout history there have been people who have lived the Micah way. As we look at these heroes, whether publicly or privately known, we will see how they have been filled with a desire to live justly and mercifully, and to see mercy and justice flourish in the lives of those around them and throughout the world. We see it in their homes, their work and their response to wider events. They are fair, they are merciful, and the world needs them so much.

We are to seek for justice when we are with our colleagues, friends and family and in all our campaigning and conversations. When we see injustice, we will try to intervene on behalf of the victims, while remembering that the perpetrators will often themselves be scared, misguided or exploited by others. In our concern for both parties, we should be aware of the risk that we may overestimate our own righteousness. Mercy and humility should always temper our justice.

Let us consider these heroes, learn from them and emulate them. When we hold justice and mercy in balance, we too can make a difference.

Reflection 34

Day 25 . . . . A call to stay loyal
Genesis 22:1-14
Romans 4:3

Centuries before Micah spoke, many centuries before Jesus walked in Judea, Abraham slowly and steadily walked up a mountain.

Jesus and all the New Testament writers would have known this story by heart. Abraham was going up the mountain to sacrifice his son, Isaac. Isaac represented all of Abraham's hopes and dreams and was the token that God's promise was going to be fulfilled. And Abraham now felt that he was being told to destroy his son and his dreams. Every step up that mountain, with Isaac chatting by his side, must have felt like torture – a torture that made no sense, that served no purpose. He was going to have to lay so much aside.

And he kept plodding up the mountain.

There are few journeys that sum up trust in God more than this one. Sometimes all that counts is the plodding; this is what the trust looks like, keeping going, trying to do what we should do, even when it is thrown back in our face, even when it seems pointless.

Abraham's loyal perseverance needed the underlying quality of courage. He had to find courage to press on through the doubts and fears, it would have been so easy to give up and to turn back.

We sometimes link perseverance with struggling through difficult times, it is good to remember that determination to keep doing what is right when life appears to be going very well can equally be a challenge.

Instinctive, even explosive, courage can be an important virtue in a crisis. That quieter courage to do each day what we have to do, through all our joys and sorrows, internal and external, is an even greater one.

Closely allied to courage is hope. Abraham trusted that God would somehow provide even in this catastrophic moment. And so he kept going up the mountain. And then the sacrifice of Isaac was not needed. Another sacrifice was provided, Abraham could begin to live his dream again. When we are trying to do what is right, nothing is pointless, nothing is wasted.

Paul wrote to the Corinthians: "We are hard pressed on every side, but not crushed; perplexed, but not in despair; persecuted, but not abandoned;

struck down, but not destroyed." And to Timothy: "I have fought the good fight, I have finished the race, I have kept the faith."

We can trust Jesus to trust us to want to persevere, and he knows how tough that sometimes is.

Reflection 35

Day 26 . . . . . . A call to forgive
Matthew 18:21-35

Paul wrote to the Ephesians "Be kind and compassionate to each other, forgiving each other just as in Christ God forgave you."

In 'The Lord's Prayer', based on the prayer Jesus taught his followers to say, people pray "Forgive us our sins, *as we forgive those who sin against us*." Jesus emphasised the point further in the story of the servant who refused to forgive a small offence even when he himself had been forgiven so much.

This may seem a hard truth but we can see the sense in it. If our hands are holding resentments against others, they will be too clenched to receive forgiveness. If we are welcomed to the party but then choose to shut the door to others, we do not understand the welcome we have been given or indeed what sort of party this is. Knowing that we are forgiven and seeing the importance of forgiveness bring such a sense of liberation and relief that surely we don't want to destroy these feelings by holding a grudge against someone else? And if we do want to hold the grudge, what does that say about our understanding of our own forgiveness?

Some things may seem too large for us to forgive, but the glimmer of *wanting* to forgive is a significant step in its own right. It shows that we don't want to hold on to this pain and resentment for ever. It shows that we are willing to recognise the intrinsic value of the other person, whatever they have done.

And that includes learning to forgive ourselves. We may need to let go of our desire to make all things well by our own strength and simply (but so hard!) to trust that Christ's power to forgive is strong enough to wash away the power of the harm that we have done and bring healing to the hurt we have caused.

Sadly, there are people whose lives have been stunted and embittered because they have not wanted to let go of the grudge they have grown accustomed to nursing.

A lack of forgiveness can become a deciding factor as to whether a couple will split up. It is the long list of silently unforgiven sins, of grudges still held, that can bring the apparently sudden end of what began as such a strong partnership. The two worlds don't usually simply drift apart; they are sometimes divided by a steadily thickening and heightening wall of unconsidered, unspoken and unforgiven resentments.

To be willing to want to forgive is to be willing to be reconciled, to be free and to set free. We are trusted to be people who want both to forgive and to be forgiven.

Reflection 36

Day 27 . . . . . .A call to love
Matthew 23:37-39
1 Corinthians 13:1-13
1 John 4:7-21

What does a life of trusting Jesus look like? Jesus said it centres on love, we are to love God and love our neighbour as we love ourselves.

Paul was later to write passionately about this. He says there is nothing more important, nothing. Love shows itself in patience and kindness and in not being envious when others have something we want. Love is not self-obsessed. It looks outwards. It is not over-bearing and certainly does not keep lists (secretly or otherwise) of the wrongs of others. It does not flare up or snap at people. It does not secretly delight when bad things happen but rejoices whenever truth, reality and goodness flourish. Love looks after others, continually wants to build good trust, keeps hope alive and keeps going, always keeps going.

Trusting Jesus involves trusting someone who believes we can love. He trusts us to want to be generous-hearted and to want the best for the other person. This does not mean smothering them, nor does it mean letting them always have their own way. It is about keeping focused on what they may need. Sometimes love needs to use tough words as well as encouraging ones. And, remembering Jesus' words about loving our neighbour as we love ourselves, we are to be likewise relentless, positive and honest in valuing ourselves.

When Jesus and Paul spoke about love they were not describing a warm and comforting feeling (although that can sometimes be a happy side effect); they were talking about deliberate choices of attitudes and behaviour. It is in the context of knowing that we are loved. "We love because he first loved us," writes John, in his old age. Holding to the truth that we are profoundly loved makes it easier to do the right thing. If you are the guest of honour at a party you will try and be polite, to say the least. You will want others to enjoy it, you will want the party to go well.

It is a challenge, but it is also very liberating because anyone can love. Circumstances, misunderstandings, missed opportunities cannot stop the ability to love. And it is very powerful. If you want to help an individual or a community then love is the deepest way to do it; love is what works, it does something profoundly powerful to the other person. Martin Luther King said this: "Hatred and bitterness can never cure the disease of fear; only love can do that. Hatred paralyses life; love releases it. Hatred confuses life; love harmonises it. Hatred darkens life; Love illumines it."

To repeat some of Paul's words in Romans 8 and extend the quotation:

> *If God is for us, who can be against us? He who did not spare his own Son, but gave him up for us all—how will he not also, along with him, graciously give us all things?... I am convinced that neither death nor life, neither angels nor demons, neither the present nor the future, nor any powers, neither height nor depth, nor anything else in all creation, will be able to separate us from the love of God that is in Christ Jesus our Lord.*

Jesus trusts us to receive love and to share love. It is the highest calling.

Reflection 37

Day 28 . . The care of the shepherd
Psalm 23,
John 10:11

This small selection of readings finishes with the twenty-third Psalm. When Jesus said "I am the good shepherd" this phrase would have reminded his listeners of this psalm, where the writer, likely King David himself, describes God as his shepherd.

Psalm 23 reads:

The Lord is my shepherd, I shall not be in
want. He makes me lie down in green pastures,
he leads me beside quiet waters,
he restores my soul.
He guides me in paths of righteousness
for his name's sake.
Even though I walk through
the valley of the shadow of death,
I will fear no evil, for you are with me;
your rod and your staff, they comfort me.

You prepare a table before me
in the presence of my enemies.
You anoint my head with oil;

my cup overflows.
Surely goodness and love will follow me
all the days of my life,
and I will dwell in the house
of the Lord for ever.

The good shepherd wishes to guide, restore, protect us from our enemies, stay with us and guard us during the darkest times, welcome us as an honoured guest and assure us of an eternal home with him.

Some people are not good at resting in the green pastures. We like being very busy, we are used to it and are shaped by it. It may raise a wry smile that the shepherd needs to 'make' us lie down, not simply gently 'suggest' we do so. A balanced life, with enough rest (one in seven waking hours is the Biblical principle) is vital to a healthy life. If we do not make use of the places of rest and refreshment – 'Sorry, I am much too busy thinking about this or that to enjoy these green pastures and quiet waters. In fact, I will turn away and pretend they don't exist. Who needs them anyway when you are as busy and important as I am' – then that is our fault, not the shepherd's.

And because he cares for us he will guide us. This might be painful, perhaps a firm nudge with the shepherd's crook will sometimes be needed to get us back on track. The aspirations are high: we are to walk in paths of righteousness, to behave well and live right, and in doing so bring honour to

God himself. Like a good courtier or ambassador being a credit to the king and his kingdom ("For his name's sake").

When we feel under great pressure and when the enemies are getting close, the shepherd has time to feast us and honour us. He worries rather less than we do. After all, he does have all the time in the world.

And through the dark valley of death itself and the surrounding grief, uncertainty and fear, he is with us and he will guide us through.

A feature of the valleys familiar to shepherds in Israel was that they were narrow and dark, twisting every few yards. One of the fears was the inevitable uncertainty of not knowing what may lie round the corner. When we go through difficult times it is often this uncertainty ('How will I cope if this happens?') that proves so difficult to face. When the event arrives we often handle it well, it is the anxious anticipation that can bring us down.

Jesus reminded his listeners that the good shepherd will sacrifice himself for the sheep and that he knows each one by name. He pointed out that there are other shepherds who will not have this sense of ultimate commitment to the flock. They may look trustworthy, but they do not care deeply and they cannot deliver what we most desire. Jesus said: "I have come that they may have life, and have it to the full" and contrasted himself with the thief who "comes only to steal and kill and destroy".

The image of the thief is a skilful and powerful one. It can be a useful test of recognising destructive influences in our lives. Who or what steals rather than gives? Who or what brings us down rather than builds up? It sometimes takes time for the victim or the perpetrator to recognise that an abusive relationship truly is abusive. As soon as that recognition happens, as soon as the 'thief' of well-being is named, then healing and confidence can begin to grow again.

And the final promise is that the shepherd will see us safely home. Surrounded by goodness, mercy and love, we will make it through.

Section 3, Evidence, Dreams and a New Beginning

Reflection 38

Doubt and history

On the twenty-ninth day I walked back up the hill.

"How was the book?" asked Thomas.

"There was much that I had not heard before and there is much I would probably enjoy thinking about. I'll try and get back to it when life is less hectic, I promise. But something I need to say now is this: in our first conversation I was thinking about my friends and those times when trust has worked and then when it hasn't. And you then bring religion and Jesus into it all. I can see and touch my friends. But I am not even sure if Jesus was real at all. Why should I think that this Jesus matters? I need some reassurance that all this actually happened."

He replied: "I have heard so many people say they are waiting for the time when their life slows down so that they can consider the serious questions. They don't seem to realise that if these really are the serious questions then it makes sense to look at them now, and not wait for an imaginary time that may or may not happen. The slower day does not always come.

"Many people do not give time to such consideration. They rush and they do and they worry but they do not always reflect. People need to take time from the busyness of actions to give time to the business of thinking. Otherwise they drift into having a view of how the world works, how they should live their lives and whom they should trust. And they do not always ask *why* they have got to this point. They have not given time to think.

"As to your doubts, that stirs rather a lot of memories; like you, I believe that evidence matters. May I share some thoughts?"

I nodded. Thomas continued:

"We make all our big decisions on the balance of probability, based on the evidence that we have. What career should I choose? Should I get married? Where should I live? There is very little in our lives that has a cast-iron guarantee. Other events may intrude and plans will change. And so we should not be disturbed that we are being asked to make a decision about faith on the balance of probability. That is how we make all our other big decisions.

"If you at all interested in Jesus then a good place to start is the historical evidence. After all, the Christian church has always claimed that the Jesus story happened in a dated, verifiable, moment in history. I learnt that sometimes I needed to learn what it is to trust the evidence even if I was not present at every moment myself. Let us go back to the first big claim that these Christians made, that this man Jesus rose from the dead.

"The resurrection is a strange thing to have made up. If I wanted to start a new religion I would not include at its core a doctrine that is so hard to believe and, if untrue, so easily disprovable. I would not include something that would lead to my imprisonment and death. Perhaps I would if I were deranged, but one of the interesting points about Christianity is that there was a wide variety of people making the same claim. This was no single person receiving 'the true faith' in a secret cave away from the eyes of others. This was a collection of men and women, in the middle of cosmopolitan, bustling Jerusalem, who claimed they had met the risen Jesus. And then others, too, said they had met this same Jesus. Their insistence that this had happened led many of them to be killed. Just over 30 years later there are enough of these resurrection-believing Christians in Rome for Nero to burn as many as he could find. Through the centuries persecution of Christians has grown, not diminished. But people still hold to this historical claim.

"People in first century Palestine knew as well as we do that dead people don't come back. But then one does, and they cannot pretend it didn't happen, despite all that would be sacrificed if they kept holding to this strange claim. It would have been much easier, attractive and safer to found a religion simply on the ethical teaching of Jesus. But that would not do justice to the facts as they saw them, so they spoke about the death and resurrection of Jesus.

"Christianity states that it is a faith rooted in history. The focus is on a person whom it is claimed lived at a specific time and place. It is therefore appropriate to use historical methods (among others, as we wish) in any exploration of its validity.

"Let us first note that there is no such thing as a neutral historical document. Every writer will have an agenda. Even a simple list of dates and events is not neutral, because someone has decided which dates to include and that decision will have involved making judgements. When historians study historical documents they do not discount them because of the views of the writer, they take these views into account as they try and work out what happened and why.

"There are four main sources of historical documents I can commend to you.

> *1) Letters* that were circulating within a few decades describing the letter-writers' views of the implications of the events. Some of these have found their way into what we now call the Bible. It is generally agreed

that they were written by Paul, Peter, James, Jude and John and one (the letter to the Hebrews) is anonymous.

2) Accounts (often called "gospels") of the life of Jesus and the immediate aftermath. These were probably not written until the second half of the first century. And the names given to the authors are Matthew, Mark, Luke (who wrote what are now called "Luke" and "Acts") and John (likely to be the same John who wrote some of the letters).

It is important not to make the mistake of thinking that just because these twenty-seven letters and accounts ended up much later in a book of sacred significance to people of a particular faith this means they lose their intrinsic historical value. These are historical documents, very old, written close to the time, and need to be treated like any other evidence.

3) Jewish documents. These events happened in Judea.

4) Roman documents. The Roman Empire included Judea.

"Let me take the first two groups of sources in one go. These writers are open about what they are trying to do. They want people to believe that Jesus was the long-awaited 'Messiah' or 'Christ', that he was divine, he was crucified, he came back to life at a particular moment in history and that he can reconcile people to God, with all that this will mean for their present and future lives.

"That is their agenda. For our purposes we focus on the two historical claims among these five, that Jesus died and 'resurrected'. The writers are right or wrong. He either did rise or he didn't. If he did not, they are lying. If we had one or two closely-associated writers hidden in a cell we may include the possibility that they were deluded, but there are too many writers writing in too many different places. There is no need for us to be generous. They are either deliberately making it up in a large and complex conspiracy or they are telling the truth. Some have argued that what they wrote was more metaphor than history, but that does not fit with the literary style of the accounts of the resurrection, let alone what the letter-writers wrote so soon afterwards. These letter-writers and gospel-writers claim that their evidence derives from eye-witness accounts, of themselves or of others. They even risk ridicule by sticking to their testimony that the first witnesses were women, which in those days would have been considered by some to invalidate their own argument. They are nailing an event to a time and place in history, describing what happened as they saw it. And it cost them their lives. People do not usually die for a metaphor.

"One example from our third source, Jewish writings, is Josephus, the key Jewish historian of the time who died in AD94. He references Jesus in the *Antiquities,* describing his death under Pilate and expressing slightly irritated surprise that people were still following him. Josephus also writes about the execution of James, brother of Jesus 'who was called Christ' and about the killing of John the Baptist.

"One example from our fourth source is the Roman historian Tacitus, describing the burning of Christians by Emperor Nero in Rome after the great fire of AD64. He feels he needs to explain to his readers who these Christians were and thus writes about Jesus' death under Pilate in the reign of Tiberius. Then, like Josephus, he writes about the unexpected twist that the death of 'Christus' seemed to provide a beginning not an end of this 'most mischievous superstition.' Suetonius similarly speaks about this new group when writing about the Roman emperors, especially Nero, but with a possible reference in his chapter on Claudius.

"We note that all of these historians in the third and fourth categories were against Christianity. They are expressing frustration that this new strange sect, founded on the person of Jesus, continued to grow. Pliny the younger's somewhat plaintive letter to Emperor Trajan in AD112 asking how to deal with the Christians in Bithynia (and Trajan's response) is a typical example.

"These sources have rightly been rigorously explored. It is possible that the Josephus extract includes later Christian amendments (additional phrases praising Jesus) but scholars feel that the original quotation contains enough specific details for this to be in harmony with the gospel accounts.

"Let us note that, even if these examples from these four groups of sources had been lost in random library fires across the Roman Empire, archaeology and other histories would still tell us that Christianity spread very fast, and that it was based on a very short public ministry by the son of a carpenter in an unfashionable northern part of Judea, who never wrote a book or led an army or ruled a country, who was then part of an intense week in Jerusalem where he was killed and then, extraordinarily, it was claimed came back to life.

"And it is the last sentence that understandably freezes historians like rabbits in the headlights. Whatever the evidence may say, many of us think we know that people don't rise from the dead. And of course people in the 1st century thought that they knew this, too.

"But note here that we have two different things going on, and this is where the question of open-mindedness comes in. Evidence, pored over by scholars, lawyers, scholars and historians, may say one thing. Our understanding of how the world works may point to another.

"And then we need to recognise a sub-division of the second point. Anthropologists will tell us that around the world and through history most people have believed in some sort of life after death. So there are some people whose understanding may lead to a preparedness to accept that once it could really have happened, in a definite, recorded, moment of history.

"But there are some whose understanding of how the world works leads them to be absolutely certain that a person who has died cannot come back to any sort of life (the early Christians did not claim it was exactly the same sort of life as before the crucifixion, they talked about resurrection, not resuscitation). If someone goes into a discussion determined to stick to their own view of how the world works, whatever the actual evidence might lead to, then this says more about how their mind works than it does about the evidence.

"Both sides need to be wary of wishful thinking. If a person wants there to be a heaven, forgiveness of sins, ultimate meaning, purpose and hope, then they are likely to want the resurrection *to have happened*. If a person does not want the possibility of the existence of God or of ultimate accountability, they are likely to want the resurrection *not* to have happened. If the resurrection did happen, then it is a game-changer. The implications can be both intensely challenging and enormously comforting. We need to be careful to remember that wishful thinking, on whatever side, is not historical evidence.

"Part of being careful is deciding not to lapse into intellectual laziness. Alex, there are people in your society today who imply that believing in Christianity is comparable to believing in unicorns or the tooth fairy. That really will not to do. The largest faith in history is not about unicorns, it is about an historical person called Jesus. Adults grow *out* of believing in the tooth fairy, but they often grow *in* to believing about Jesus. History is different from imaginative story. A serious enquirer will want to test the evidence, not run away from it.

"It is important to note that the early Christian writers did not make things easy for themselves. Nowhere did they claim that this was some immeasurable 'he lives in your heart, his values live on' sort of resurrection. They kept talking about a bodily resurrection at a particular time and place. They opened themselves up to the possibility of easy refutation and rebuttal. But no-one seemed able to refute or rebut them. Considering how many people hated, feared and despised them, this lack of a successful response is in itself interesting to the historian.

"And remember that the historical evidence is only one reason why it is rational and thoughtful to think that there may indeed be something in all this talk about God. There are many other pointers. Keep thinking, keep asking. Follow the thoughts home."

He got up and walked across the glade. I was sitting against my old familiar tree in the afternoon sun. I began to doze off and soon I was in a dream.

Reflection 39

*Playing in an orchestra,
returning to the hall*

The hill has faded and my dream takes me into a large room, where I have been invited to play second clarinet in the orchestra. I do not know much about the orchestra except that it has been around a long time.

I am not yet sure how long the concert will be or how the music needs to be played; I do not yet know the speed, variations or volume.

I understand that the first violinist will be the leader, taking, as happens in small ensembles, the role of the conductor. But it does not seem like a small ensemble, I am not quite sure how large the orchestra is; perhaps some trick of the lighting makes it hard to discern, but, glancing around, I sense that the numbers sweep far back all around me.

I get ready to play.

The first oboe leans over and whispers: "I've heard that our leader is not only a very good violinist, but was also involved in the composing. Perhaps this time we will know how the music is really meant to sound."

Before the music begins the first violinist goes round the orchestra. There is a word here and a smile there. It seems he knows all the players. One or two adjust their music stands or look at the floor and appear to want to avoid contact. Sometimes he speaks quietly, sometimes he laid a hand on a shoulder. With one he reaches out and lifts up his head so they are looking at each other. I cannot quite hear what is being said to the others. He comes over to me.

I quickly realise that he knows what other orchestras I have joined, how long I have played the clarinet, the times when I have made good progress and the times I stopped practising and made no progress at all. He even knows about the time when I broke my clarinet and stormed off in a huff. It is all a little unsettling, but somehow reassuring. He knows all about me, but he still wants me there.

It takes time for the leader to go round the orchestra but the concert still begins on time. When the music starts I notice that he is often looking at other players while still playing himself. The music is sometimes slow and sometimes fast, but he never seems to be rushed.

It is a prestigious orchestra. I had needed a new clarinet, this had been bought for me. I needed a new suit, this was provided. It even crossed my mind whether it is the first violinist who had organised it all for everyone and met the cost. If so, my earlier thought was right, he wants me there. And, as he looks across at me, I wondered if perhaps he not only *wants* me in the orchestra, but he *likes* having me in the orchestra. It matters to him that I am there.

There are some in the orchestra whom I am rather surprised to see, I had not realised that they were the sort of people who might feel part of this. But then I realised I was not quite sure what 'sort' of people this was for. Perhaps the invitations went wider than I thought. I smiled to myself as I realised that they might be as surprised to see me as I was to see them. He not only wants me, he wants them.

The first violinist sometimes speaks to the whole orchestra and sometimes to individuals. He points out difficult parts of the score, knowing where people need guidance. He warns against complacency when sections appear easy. He counsels perseverance when the music is difficult.

The music continues. There are disagreements: two cellists nearly come to blows. A trumpeter gets some notes wrong. I want to do my best but often miss the timing. Through it all the first violinist plays calmly. He sometimes walks around whilst playing, encouraging with a word or a smile, keeping the music going.

I become a little irritated with the flautist to my right. She seems to be getting the more tuneful part in this section and her notes go right through my head. People are smiling, everything seems to be just fine for her. I don't want to do anything dramatic so I edge forward slightly, bend down to pick up an imaginary object, and as I move my hand back up I nudge her music stand, just hard enough for the page of music to fall off.

I shrug, as if I am sorry but really have more important things to think about. Glancing up, I realised that the first violinist is looking directly at me. I suddenly wish I had not been so childish. The violinist shakes his head, slightly sadly, but then nods gently. I realise he wants me to keep playing, that I am free to stay and I am free to play.

At the next pause I apologise fulsomely to the flautist. She is very kind and I feel as if I have somehow been welcomed by her and by the first violinist to a new beginning.

A young man gets up from his place in the orchestra. "There is much about being here that I like," he says "but I would rather play with other conductors. Some of this is okay, but I want to pick and mix my experiences." The leader of the orchestra does not rush over and force him back into his seat. "You are free to go," he says sadly, "You have the freedom to make that choice. You are always welcome back."

There is a moment when I look over and realise that the first violinist has his eyes shut. He appears to be concentrating hard. I whisper to my friend the oboist: "He takes this music very seriously. "Yes," she replies, "and he is not only thinking about the music, he is thinking about us."

I glance at the music stand of a neighbour, another second clarinettist. I notice that his score is not quite the same as mine and wonder if every person in the orchestra has their own part to play.

The leader moves his bow and his sleeve rides up his arm. He is quite badly scarred.

***

The dream took me back to the glade, and the trees were reaching up and over, their branches forming a canopy, even a roof, and I realise I am now in a hall and wearing strange clothes. The only light is from a fire on the floor in the middle and my eyes take time to adjust. I have been listening to the quiet exchange between King Edwin and his advisor. I watch the smoke from the fire make its way up and through the hole in the roof while the chatter of friends, lords and servants fade in the background. It is the warm and relaxed stage after the feast that so often brings comfort and peace. There has not yet been a minstrel song or tale tonight, instead we have listened to the visitor, Paulinus. That interrupted all the normal expectations of the evening but a glance from King Edwin has always been enough to silence even the most revelled of thegns. I had not followed all of visitor's words but as I look again at the smoke disappearing to the sky beyond the hall I remember the conversation about the sparrow.

I imagine myself back into Saxon times: the certainties of the Western Roman Empire had faded two centuries before. In their wake have come settlers, invaders, new learning and new stories. There have been Christians in the land for five centuries, but I know little about them. Here is Paulinus asking the king, us, me, to trust in their Christ. I think back to the sadness of the last year, with death in the family; I remember the feud over the bracelet (it is strange what lusts are raised by such things). I glance across at Edwin. Even kings must have their burdens and their fears.

Perhaps it was worth waiting before the minstrel began. Listening to Paulinus before the saga or song had not taken up too much time. Perhaps there really is something here to consider. Five hundred years is a long time, after all. These have been uncertain centuries but here we are, still talking about this man from Galilee or whatever that place was called. Who would have thought that Roman power would have fallen? What is it about this man that people are still talking about him? I look at the fire and smile. Not many stories have lasted this long. I wonder if it will keep going.

Reflection 40

Returning home

I awoke, slightly uncomfortable with the tree unyielding behind me. I got up from the grass and began to walk, slightly nervously, to one of the groups. I joined in with the conversations about maps and food, weather and routes, about who can carry which bags at which times. Whether anyone will need to be carried. They then tell me that my journey is with the group going in the direction of my village, that we would walk together until I got home.

We did so, and when I arrived I went back into my study. I sat in my old chair and allowed thoughts to dance around my mind. Familiar faces gather round me. Faces from childhood, from recent years and from the present. Faces of people I have trusted and I trust.

It dawned on me that I need to understand trust not just for my own sake but because trusting relationships make such a difference to friendships, communities, workplaces and families. I need to be looking outwards, not inwards. Such things are caught more than taught. If my friends and I can model good trust, we change the world.

Trusting someone who cares, trusting someone who can help, trusting someone who trusts me. Am I able to trust the right people and the right ideas? Switching it round, am I able to be worthy of trust for someone else?

I think about Thomas. If I meet him again I must ask more about his story and why this means so much to him. He is quite passionate about it all. And suddenly I have an image of a locked room in a town far away, an unexpected arrival, an astonished face, hands reaching out and words of acclamation.

I picture a sparrow flying through a hall. It comes in at one end and flies out the other. A king considers deeply, people tell the story, an historian writes richly. People's lives are changed.

And an orchestra keeps playing.

And a man walking through a small town named Jericho calls a tax collector down from a tree and changes his life.

I notice the half-formed, half-forgotten, poem pushed to the side. I move it back to the centre of the desk.

> *There are times when I long*
> *For a world refreshed*
> *With hope restored, renewed*

Where truth and trust grow strong
Once more
And fear is lost in love

And I wonder if I have the courage to turn the hope into a response, the longing into a journey.